Machine Learning with Python

The Ultimate Guide to Learn Machine Learning Algorithms. Includes a Useful Section about Analysis, Data Mining and Artificial Intelligence in Business Applications.

content within this book has been derived from various sources. Please consult a licensed professional before attempting any techniques outlined in this book.

By reading this document, the reader agrees that under no circumstances is the author responsible for any losses, direct or indirect, which are incurred as a result of the use of information contained within this document, including, but not limited to, — errors, omissions, or inaccuracies.

Table of Contents

Introduction

Congratulations on purchasing *Machine Learning with Python - The Ultimate Guide to Learn Machine Learning Algorithms. Includes a Useful Section about Analysis, Data Mining and Artificial Intelligence in Business Applications* and thank you for doing so.

The following chapters will discuss the fundamental concepts of Artificial Intelligence, Machine Learning and Data Mining in the light of Python programming language to help you understand the process of creating a data pipeline for the machine learning model. You will start this book by developing a solid understanding of the basics of the artificial intelligence technology and data mining. It is important to master the concepts of artificial intelligence technology and learn how researchers are breaking the boundaries of data science to mimic human intelligence in machines. The power of artificial intelligence has already started to manifest in our environment and in our everyday objects. This chapter will also discuss the benefits of using data mining technology, the challenges facing the data mining technology and learn about some data mining tools that you can leverage for your business. The basic concepts of machine learning, namely, "representation," "optimization" and "evaluation" along with an overview of different types of machine learning algorithms can be found in the second chapter. You will also learn about ten different supervised and unsupervised learning algorithms in exquisite detail.

In Chapter 3, you will find instructions on how to install Python on your operating systems (Windows, Mac, and Linux). The concept of Python data types is presented in exquisite detail with various examples of each data type. In Python, variables are at the heart of every syntax. You will learn how to create these variables and assign the desired data type to them. It will introduce you to the basic concepts of writing efficient and effective Python codes, focusing on various programming elements such as Booleans, Tuples, Sets, Dictionaries and much more. Each concept is explained with standard syntax and relevant examples.

The last chapter will provide you an overarching guide for everything you need to know for successful development and training of neural network models using one of the most popular machine learning libraries called "TensorFlow." The end-to-end example described in this chapter will allow you to run a simultaneous hands-on exercise to develop your first neural network model using the open-source TensorFlow platform. You will also learn predictive analysis in explicit detail as well as various applications of machine learning and Artificial Intelligence to resolve everyday business problems.

There are plenty of books on this subject on the market, thanks again for choosing this one! Every effort was made to ensure it is full of as much useful information as possible; please enjoy!

Chapter 1: Artificial Intelligence and Data Science Technologies

Human beings or Homo Sapiens, often tout themselves as being the most superior species to have ever housed the planet Earth, ascribing primarily to their "intelligence." Even the most complex animal behavior is never considered as intelligent; however, the simplest of human behavior is ascribed to intelligence. For example, when a female digger wasp returns with food to her burrow, she deposits the food on the threshold and checks for intruders prior to carrying her food inside. Sounds like quite the intelligent wasp, right? However, when we look at an experiment conducted on these wasps, where the scientist displaced the food not too far from the entrance of the burrow while the wasp was inside, we realize that the wasps continued to reiterate the whole procedure every time the food was moved from its original location. This experiment concluded that inability of the wasp to adapt to the changing circumstances and thereby "intelligence," is noticeably absent in the wasps. Therefore, what is this "human intelligence?" Psychologists characterize human intelligence as a composite of multiple abilities such as learning from experiences and being able to adapt accordingly, understanding abstract concepts, reasoning, problem-solving, use of language and perception.

The science of developing human-controlled and operated machinery, such as digital computers or robots that can mimic human intelligence, adapt to new inputs and perform human-like tasks is called "Artificial Intelligence" (AI). Thanks to Hollywood, most people think of robots coming to life and wreaking havoc on the planet, when they hear the words Artificial Intelligence. That is far from the truth. The core principle of Artificial Intelligence is the ability of the AI-powered machines to rationalize (think like humans) and take actions (mimic human actions) towards fulfilling the targeted goal. Simply put, Artificial Intelligence is the creation of a machine that will think and act like humans. The three paramount goals of Artificial Intelligence are learning, reasoning and perception.

Although the term Artificial Intelligence was coined in 1956, the British pioneer of Computer Sciences, Alan Mathison Turing, performed groundbreaking work in the field of Artificial Intelligence, in the mid-20th century. In 1935, Turing developed an abstract computing machine with a scanner and unlimited memory in the form of symbols. The scanner was capable of moving back and forth through the memory, reading the existing symbols as well as writing further symbols of the memory. A programming instruction would dictate the actions of the scanner and was stored in the memory. Thus, Turing generated a machine with implicit learning capabilities that could modify and improve its own programming. This concept is widely known as the universal "Turing Machine" and serves as a basis for all modern computers. Turing claimed that computers could learn from their own experience and solve problems using a guiding principle known as "heuristic problem-solving."

In 1950s, the early AI research was focused on problem-solving and symbolic methods. By the 1960s, the AI research had a major leap of interest from "The US Department of Defense," who started working towards training computers to mirror human reasoning. In the 1970s, the "Defense Advanced Research Projects Agency" (DARPA) has successfully completed its street mapping projects. It might come to you as a surprise, that DARPA actually produced intelligent personal assistants in 2003, long before the existence of the famous Siri and Alexa. This groundbreaking work in the field of AI has paved the way for automation and reasoning observed in the modern-day computers.

Here are the core human traits that we aspire to mimic in the machines:

1. **Knowledge** – In order for machines to be able to act and react like humans, they require an abundance of data and

information pertaining to the world around us. To be able to implement knowledge engineering AI must have seamless access to data objects, data categories and data properties as well as the relationship between them that can be managed and stored in the data storages.

2. **Learning** – Of all the different forms of learning applicable to AI, the simplest one is "trial and error" method. For example, a chess learning computer program will try all possible moves until the mate-in-one move is found to end the game. The program to be used the next time it encounters the same position then stores this move. This relatively easy to implement an aspect of learning called "rote learning," involves simple memorization of individual items and procedures. The most challenging part of the learning is called "generalization," which involves applying the past experience to the corresponding new scenarios.

3. **Problem solving** – The systematic process to reach a predefined goal or solution by searching through a range of possible actions can be defined as problem solving. The problem-solving techniques can be customized for a particular problem or used for a wide variety of problems. A general-purpose problem-solving method frequently used in AI is "means-end analysis," which involves a step-

by-step deduction of the difference between the current state and final state of the goal. Think about some of the basic functions of a robot, back and forth movement or picking up stuff that leads to the fulfillment of a goal.

4. **Reasoning** – The act of reasoning can be defined as the ability to draw inferences that are appropriate to the given situation. The two forms of reasoning are called "deductive reasoning" and "inductive reasoning." In deductive reasoning, if the premise is true then the conclusion is assumed to be true. On the other hand, in inductive reasoning, even if the premise is true, the conclusion may or may not be true. Although considerable success has been achieved in programming computers to perform deductive reasoning, the implementation of "true reasoning" remains aloof and one of the biggest challenges facing Artificial Intelligence.

5. **Perception** – The process of generating a multidimensional view of an object by means of various sensory organs can be defined as perception. This creation of awareness of the environment is complicated by a number of factors, such as the viewing angle, the direction and intensity of the light and the amount of contrast produced by the object, with the surrounding field. Breakthrough developments have been made in the field

of artificial perception and can be easily observed in our daily life with the advent of self-driving cars and robots that can collect empty soda cans while moving through the buildings.

Importance of Artificial Intelligence

To get a sense of how important Artificial Intelligence is in our daily lives, it would be easier to state what part of our modern lifestyle has not been touched by it. The "intelligent machines" designed to augment human capabilities and enhance efficiencies are influencing every facet of human life. Artificial Intelligence is the central tenet of the Fourth Industrial Revolution that could potentially dispute our ideas about what it means to be "human."

Here are few reasons to help you understand with Artificial Intelligence is important for your business right now:

- Automation of repetitive learning and discovery from data. Unlike hardware-driven robotic automation that tends to automate manual tasks, AI performs high frequency, high volume, and computer-based tasks constantly and reliably. However, for the AI automation, the human inquiry continues to be necessary to set up the system and ask pertinent questions.

- Adding intelligence to already available products. The way Siri was added to the new generation of iPhones, AI would also be used to enhance the capabilities of products that we already use. It is impossible to sell AI as a self only application. Technologies at home and in the workplace, like investment analysis or network security, can be improved significantly by combining a large amount of data with automation, smart machines, robots and conversational platforms.

- Progressive learning algorithms will help AI adapt to the changing world. Machine learning allows the program to learn, take note and improve upon its errors. To aid the algorithm is acquiring skills; AI finds structure and patterns in the data, making the algorithm function as a classifier or a predictor. Similar to how the algorithm has taught itself how to play chess, it can also teach itself what online products should be recommended next. The beauty of this model is that it adapts with every new set of data. If the first response is deemed incorrect, an AI technique called back propagation allows the model to adjust using the new available date and training.

- AI is making an analysis of a deeper and larger data set with the use of neural networks containing multiple hidden layers. Think about it fraud detection system with multiple hidden layers could only be built in a dream just a few years ago. With the advent of big data and never before imagined computer powers, a completely new world awaits us. Data to the machines is like the gas to your vehicles, the more data you can feed them, the results are faster and accurate. Deep learning models thrive on excess of data because they learn directly from the data.

- Unbelievable accuracy has been achieved through the deep neural networks of the AI. For example, the more we use Alexa and Google Search, the more accurate they become because they are based on deep learning. These deep neural networks are also empowering our medical field. Image classification and object recognition are now capable of finding cancer on MRIs with similar accuracy as that of a highly trained radiologist.

- AI helps to bring out the best out of the data. Today data is its own currency and when algorithms are self-learning it can easily become intellectual property. The raw data is like a gold mine, the more and deeper you dig, the more gold that is the useful information you can dig out. Simply applying AI to the data can help you get to the right answers faster and makes for a competitive advantage. Remember the best data will always win, even though everybody is using similar techniques.

- Rapid implementation of AI technologies is allowing new technologies to be introduced at an incredibly fast pace and can be difficult to keep up with. It is becoming increasingly important for more people to truly understand all of the implications AI can have on our world.

- The impact of AI on our society cannot be underestimated. As we expand the reach and application of AI in the world around us, it is sure to improve, transform or create things that we can still not imagine.

- Technology giants like "Google" and "Amazon," are heavily investing in AI research and development, which goes to show the importance AI holds for businesses in general and by extension, the whole economy.

- AI will lead to legal implications across the globe, with nations requiring reviewing and update their laws and regulations in the light of AI policies. The use of AI in healthcare and transportation will require enhances government scrutiny of the protected information being used by AI.

- Strong collaboration between Private and Public Sectors across the globe and not just the large tech companies is essential to successfully implement AI to better serve humanity. Our travel and hotel industries are already going through this revolution.

Data Mining

Data mining can be defined as "the process of exploring and analyzing large volumes of data to gather meaningful patterns and rules." Data mining falls under the umbrella of data science and is heavily used to build artificial intelligence-based machine learning models, for example, search engine algorithms. Although the process of "digging through data" to uncover hidden patterns and predict future events has been around for a long time and referred to as "knowledge discovery in databases," the term "Data mining" was coined as recently as the 1990s.

Data mining consists of three foundational and highly intertwined disciplines of science, namely, "statistics" (the mathematical study of data relationships), "machine learning algorithms" (algorithms that can be trained with an inherent capability to learn) and "artificial intelligence" (machines that can display human-like intelligence). With the advent of the big data, the Data mining technology has been evolved to keep up with the "limitless potential of big data" and affordable computing power. The once considered tedious, labor-intensive and time-consuming activities have been automated using advance processing speed and power of the modern computing systems.

"Data mining is the process of finding anomalies, patterns and correlations within large data sets to predict outcomes. Using a

broad range of techniques, you can use this information to
increase revenues, cut costs, improve customer relationships,
reduce risks and more."
– SAS

According to SAS, "unstructured data alone makes up 90% of the digital universe." This avalanche of big data does not necessarily guarantee more knowledge. The application of data mining technology allows filtering of all the redundant and unnecessary data noise to garner the understanding of relevant information that can be used in the immediate decision-making process.

Applications of Data Mining

The applications of data mining technology are everywhere, ranging from retail pricing and promotions to credit risk assessment by financial institutions and banks. Every industrial sector is benefiting from the applications the data mining technology. Here are some of the examples of industrial applications and data mind technology:

Healthcare Bioinformatics

To predict the likelihood of the patient suffering from one or more health conditions given the risk factors, healthcare professionals use statistical models. Genetically transferred diseases can be prevented or mediated from the onset of deteriorating health conditions, by modeling the patient's genetic, family and demographic data. In developing nations, there is a scarcity of healthcare professionals; therefore, assisted diagnoses and prioritization of patients is very critical. Data mining-based models have recently been deployed in such countries to help with the prioritization of patients before healthcare professionals can reach these countries and administer treatment.

Credit Risk Management

Financial institutions and banks deploy data mining models to predict the likelihood of a potential credit card customer failing to make their credit payments on time as well as to determine appropriate credit limit that the customer may qualify for. These data mining models collect and extract information from a variety of input sources including personal information, Financial history of the customer at and demographic among other sources. The model then provides the institution or bank interest rate to be collected from the client based on the assessed risk. For example, Data mining models take the credit score of the applicant into consideration and individuals with a low credit score are given the highest interest rates.

Spam Filtering

Many email clients such as "Google mail" and "Yahoo mail" rely on the data mining tools to detect and flag email spam and malware. By analyzing hundreds and thousands of shared characteristics of spams and malware, the data mining tool provides insight that can be used in the development of enhanced security measures and tools. These applications are not only capable of detecting spam, but they are also very efficient in categorizing the spam emails and storing them in a separate folder, so they never enter the user's inbox.

Marketing

Retail companies have an incessant need to understand their customer demands and expectations. With the use of data mining tools, businesses can analyze customer-related data such as purchase history, demographics, gender, age, and any other important identifying information to gather valuable customer insights and segment them into groups based on shared shopping attributes. Companies then devise unique marketing strategies and campaigns to target specific groups, such as discount offers and promotions both in-store and online through various mediums of marketing such as flyers in the mail, coupons at the store, or discounts on phone apps.

Sentiment Analysis

With the use of a technique called "text mining," companies can analyze their data from all of their social media platforms to understand the "sentiment" of their customer base. This process of understanding the feelings of a big group of people towards a particular topic is called "sentiment analysis" and can be carried out using data mining tools. With the use of pattern recognition technology, input data from social media platforms and other related public content websites are collected using the "text mining" technology and identify data patterns that feed into a general understanding of the topic. To further dive into this data, the "natural language processing" technique can be used to understand the human language in a specific context.

Qualitative Data Mining

The "text mining" technique can also be used to perform quantitative research and gain insight from large volumes of unstructured data. Recently a research study conducted by the University of Berkeley revealed the use of data mining models and child welfare program studies.

Product Recommendation Systems

Advance "recommendations systems" are like the bread and butter for online retailers. The use of predictive customer behavior analysis is rising among small and large online businesses to gain a competitive edge in the market. Some of the largest e-commerce businesses including" Amazon," Macy's" and" Nordstrom" have invested millions of dollars in the development of their own proprietary data mining models to forecast market trends and all for a more engaging in enhanced user experience to their customers. The on-demand entertainment giant "Netflix" bought over million dollars' worth algorithm to enhance the accuracy of their video recommendation system, which reportedly increased the recommendation accuracy for "Netflix" by over 8%.

The Data Mining Process

The most widely used data mining processes can be broken down into six steps as listed below:

1. Business understanding

It is very critical to understand the project goals and what is it that you are trying to achieve through the data mining process. Companies always start with the establishment of a defined goal and a project plan that includes details such as individual team member roles and responsibility, project milestones, project timelines, and key performance indicators and metrics.

2. Data understanding

Data is available from a wide variety of input sources and in different formats. With the use of data visualization tools, the data properties and features, you be assessed to ensure the existing data set is able to meet the established business requirements and project goals.

3. Data preparation

The preprocessing of Data collected in multiple formats is very important. The data set must be scrubbed to remove data redundancies and identify gaps before it is deemed appropriate for mining. Considering the amount of data to be analyzed, the data pre-processing and processing steps can take a long time. To enhance the speed of the data mining process, instead of using a single system company prefer using distributed systems as part of their "database management systems." The distributed systems also provide enhanced security measures by segregating the data into multiple devices rather than a single data warehouse. At this stage, it is also very crucial to account for backup options and failsafe measures in the event of data loss during the data manipulation stage.

4. Data modeling

Applicable mathematical models and analytical tools are applied to the data set to identify patterns.

5. Evaluation

The modeling results and data patterns are evaluating against the project goal and objectives to determine if the data findings can be released for use across the organization.

6. Deployment

Once the insights gathered from the data has been evaluated as applicable to the functioning and operations of the organization; these insights can be shared across the company to be included in its day-to-day operations. With the use of a Business Intelligence tool, the data findings can be stored at a centralized location and accessed using the BI tool as needed.

Pros of Data Mining

Automated Decision-Making

With the use of data mining technology, businesses can seamlessly automate tedious manual tasks and analyze large volumes of data to gather insights for the routine and critical decision-making process. For example, financial lending institutions, banks and online payment services use data mining technology to detect potentially fraudulent transactions, verify user identity and ensure data privacy to protect their customers against identity theft. When company's operational algorithms are working in coordination with the data mining models, a company can independently gather, analyze, and take actions on data to improve and streamline their operational decision-making process.

Accurate Prediction and Forecasting

Project planning is fundamental to the success of any company. Managers and executives can leverage data mining technology to gather reliable forecasts and predictions on future market trends and include in their future planning process. For example, one of the leading retail company "Macys" has implemented demand forecasting models to generate reliable demand forecasts for Mary is clothing categories at individual stores, in order to increase the efficiency of their supply chain by routing the forecasted inventory to each store and cater to the needs of the market more efficiently.

Cost Reduction

With the help of data mining technologies companies can maximize the use of their resources by smarty allocating them across the business model. The use of data mining technology in planning as well as an automated decision-making process results in accurate forecasts leading to significant cost reductions. For example, a major airline company "Delta" implemented RFID chips inside their passengers checked-in baggage and gathered baggage handling data that was analyzed using data mining technology to identify improvement opportunities in their process and minimizing the number of mishandled baggage. This not only resulted in a cost saving on the search and rerouting process of the lost baggage but also translated into higher customer satisfaction.

Customer Insights

Companies across different industrial sectors have deployed Data mining models to gather valuable insights from existing customer data, which can be used to segment and target customers with similar shopping attributes using similar marketing strategies and campaigns. Customer personas can be created using the data mining technology to provide a more engaging and personalized user experience to the customer. For example, "Disney" has recently invested over a billion dollars to develop and deploy "Magic bands," offering the convenience and enhanced experience and Disney resorts. At the same time, these bands can be used to collect data on patron activities and interactions with different "Disney" products and services at the park to further enhance the "Disney experience."

"When [data mining and] predictive analytics are done right, the analyses aren't a means to a predictive end; rather, the desired predictions become a means to analytical insight and discovery. We do a better job of analyzing what we really need to analyze and predicting what we really want to predict."
– Harvard Business Review Insight Center Report

Challenges of Data Mining

1. Big data

Our digital life has inundated companies with large volumes of data, which is estimated to reach 1.7 MB per second per person by 2020. This exponential increase in volume and complexity of big data has presented challenges for the data mining technology. Companies are looking to expedite their decision-making process by swiftly, efficiently extracting, and analyzing data to gain valuable insights from their data treasure trove. The ultimate goal of the data mining technology is to overcome these challenges and unlock the true potential of data value. The "4Vs" of big data namely velocity, variety, volume and veracity represent the four major challenges facing the data mining technology.

The skyrocketing "velocity" or speed at which new data is being generated poses a challenge of increasing storage requirements. The "variety" or different data types collected and stored require advance data mining capabilities to be able to simultaneously process a multitude of data formats. Data mining tools that are not equipped to process such highly variable big data provide low value, due to their inefficiency and analyzing unstructured and structured data together.

The large volume of big data is not only challenging for storage but it is even more challenging do identify correct data in a timely manner, owing to a massive reduction in the speed of the data mining tools and algorithms. To add on to this challenge, the data "veracity" denoting that not all of the collected data is accurate and can be incomplete or even biased. The data mining tools are struggling to deliver high-quality results in a timely manner by analyzing high quantity or big data.

2. Overloading models

Data models that describe the natural errors of the data set instead of the underlying patterns are often "over-fitted" or overloaded. These models tend to be highly complex and the choir a large number of independent media bowls to precisely predict a future event. Data volume and variety further increase the risk of overloading. A high number of variables tend to restrict the data model within the confines of the known sample data. On the other hand, an insufficient number of variables can compromise the relevance of the model. To obtain the required number of variables for the data mining models, to be able to strike a balance between the accuracy of the results and the prediction capabilities, is one of the major challenges facing the data mining technology today.

3. Data privacy and security

To cater to the large volume of big data generated on a daily basis, companies are investing in cloud-based storage servers along with its on premise servers. The cloud computing technology is relatively new in the market and the inherent nature of this service poses multiple security and privacy concerns. Data privacy and security is one of the biggest concerns of the Smart consumers who are willing to take their business to the company that can promise them security of their personal information and data. This requires organizations to evaluate their customer relationship and prioritize the customer privacy over the development of policies that can potentially compromise customer data security.

4. Scaling costs

With increasing speed of data generation leading to high volume of complex data, organizations are required to expand their data mining models and deploy them across the organization. To unlock the full potential of data mining tools, companies are required to heavily invest in computing infrastructure and processing power to efficiently run the data mining models. Big-ticket item purchases including data servers, software, and advance computers must be made in order to scale the analytical capabilities of the organization.

Data Mining Trends

Increased Computing Speed

With increasing volume and complexity of big data, Data mining tools need more powerful and faster computers to efficiently analyze data. The existing statistical techniques like "clustering" art equipment to process only thousands of input data with a limited number of variables. However, companies are gathering over millions of new data observations with hundreds of variables making the analysis too complicated for the computing system to process. The big data is going to continue to explode, demanding super computers that are powerful enough to rapidly and efficiently analyze the growing big data.

Language Standardization

The data science community is actively looking to standardize a language for the data mining process. This ongoing effort will allow the analyst to conveniently work with a variety of data mining platforms by mastering one standard Data mining language.

Scientific Mining

The success of data mining technology in the industrial world has caught the eye of the scientific and academic research community. For example, psychologists are using "association analysis" to capture her and identify human behavioral patterns for research purposes. Economists are using protective analysis algorithms to forecast future market trends by analyzing current market variables.

Web Mining

Web mining can be defined as "the process of discovering hidden data patterns and chains using similar techniques of data mining and applying them directly on the Internet." The three main types of web mining are "content mining," "usage mining" and "structure mining." For example, "Amazon" uses web mining to gain an understanding of customer interactions with their website and mobile application, to provide more engaging and enhanced user experience to their customers.

Data Mining Tools

Some of the most widely used data mining tools are:

Orange

Orange is an "open-source component-based software written in Python." It is most frequently used for basic data mining analysis and offers top-of-the-line data pre-processing features.

RapidMiner

RapidMiner is an "open-source component-based software written in Java." It is most frequently used for "predictive analysis" and offers integrated environments for "machine learning," "deep learning" and "text mining."

Mahout

Mahout is an open-source platform primarily used for unsupervised learning process" and developed by "Apache." It is most frequently used to develop "machine learning algorithms for clustering, classification and collaborative filtering." This software requires advanced knowledge and expertise to be able to leverage the full capabilities of the platform.

MicroStrategy

MicroStrategy is a "business intelligence and data analytics software that can complement all data mining models." This platform offers a variety of drivers and gateways to seamlessly connect with any enterprise resource and analyze complex big data by transforming it into accessible visualizations that can be easily shared across the organization.

Chapter 2: Machine Learning Algorithms

The notion of Artificial Intelligence Technology is derived from the idea that computers can be engineered to exhibit human-like intelligence and mimic human reasoning and learning capacities, adapting to fresh inputs and performing duties without needing human intervention. The principle of artificial intelligence encompasses machine learning. Machine Learning Technology (ML) refers to the principle of Artificial Intelligence Technology, which focuses mainly on the designed ability of computers to learn explicitly and self-train, identifying information patterns to enhance the underlying algorithm and making autonomous decisions without human involvement. In 1959, the term "machine learning" was coined during his tenure at IBM, by the pioneering gaming and artificial intelligence professor, Arthur Samuel.

Machine learning hypothesizes that contemporary computers can be trained using targeted training data sets, which can readily be tailored to create required functionality. Machine learning is guided by a pattern recognition method where previous interactions and outcomes are recorded and revisited in a way that corresponds to its present position. Because machines are needed to process infinite volumes of data, with fresh data constantly flowing in, they need to be equipped to adapt to the fresh data without being programmed by a person, considering the iterative aspect of machine learning. Machine learning has close relations with the field of Statistics, which is focused on generating predictions using advanced computing tools and technologies. The research of "mathematical optimization" provides the field of machine learning with techniques, theories, and implementation areas. Machine learning is also referred to as "predictive analytics" in its implementation to address business issues. In ML, the "target" is known as "label" while in statistics it is called "dependent variable." A "variable" in statistics is known as "feature" in ML. In addition, a "feature creation" in ML is known as "transformation" in statistics.

ML technology is also closely related to data mining and optimization. ML and data mining often utilize the same techniques with considerable overlap. ML focuses on generating predictions based on predefined characteristics of the given training data. On the other hand, data mining pertains to the identification of unknown characteristics in large volumes of data. Data mining utilizes many techniques of ML, but with distinct objectives; similarly, machine learning also utilizes techniques of data mining through the "unsupervised learning algorithms" or as a pre-processing phase to enhance the prediction accuracy of the model. The intersection of these two distinct research areas stems from the fundamental assumptions with which they operate. In machine learning, efficiency is generally assessed with regard to the capacity of the model to reproduce known knowledge, while in "knowledge discovery and information mining (KDD)" the main job is to discover new information. An "uninformed or unsupervised" technique, evaluated in terms of known information, will be easily outperformed by other "supervised techniques." On the contrary, "supervised techniques" cannot be used in a typical "KDD" task owing to the lack of training data.

Data optimization is another area that machine learning is closely linked with. Various learning issues can be formulated as minimization of certain "loss function" on the training data set. "Loss functions" are derived as the difference between the predictions generated by the model being trained and the input data values the distinction between the two areas stems from the objective of "generalization." Optimization algorithms are designed to decrease the loss on the training data set; the objective of machine learning is to minimize the loss of input data from the real world.

Machine learning has become such a "heated" issue that its definition varies across the world of academia, corporate companies, and the scientific community. Here are some of the commonly accepted definitions from select sources that are extremely known:

- *"Machine learning is based on algorithms that can learn from data without relying on rules-based programming."* – McKinsey.

- *"Machine Learning at its most basic is the practice of using algorithms to parse data, learn from it, and then make a determination or prediction about something in the world."* – NVidia

- *"The field of Machine Learning seeks to answer the question, how can we build computer systems that automatically improve with experience, and what are the fundamental laws that govern all learning processes?"* – Carnegie Mellon University

- *"Machine learning is the science of getting computers to act without being explicitly programmed."* – Stanford University

Core Concepts of Machine Learning

Today there are several kinds of ML, but the notion of ML is mainly based on three components "representation," "evaluation" and "optimization." Here are some of the standard concepts that are applicable to all of them:

Representation

Machine learning models cannot directly hear, see or sense input examples. A data representation is therefore needed to provide a helpful vantage point for the model in the main data attributes. The choice of significant characteristics that best represent data is very essential to train a machine learning model effectively.

"Representation" simply refers to the act of "representing" data points to computer in a language that it understands using a set of classifiers. A classifier may be defined as "a model that inputs a vector of discrete and/or ongoing function values and outputs a single discrete value called "class." To learn from the represented data, a model must have the desired classifier in the training data set or "hypothesis space" that you want the models to be trained on. The data features used to represent the input are very critical to the machine learning system. Any "classifier" that is external to the hypothesis space cannot be learned by the model. For developing a required machine learning model, data characteristics are so essential that it can easily be the difference between successful and unsuccessful machine learning projects.

A training data set with several independent "features," which are well linked to the "class," can make learning much easier for the machine. On the other side, it may not be easy for the machine to learn from the class with complex functions. This often requires the processing of the raw data so that the desired features for the ML model can be built from it. The method of deriving features from raw data set tends to be the ML project's most time-consuming and laborious component. It is also considered the most creative and interesting part of the project where intuition and "trial and error" play just as important a role as the technical requirements. The ML process is not a "one shot" process of developing and executing a training data set, but an iterative process requiring analysis of the post-execution output, followed by modification of the training data set. Domain specificity is another reason why the training dataset requires comprehensive time and effort. Training data set to produce predictions based on consumer behavior analysis for an e-commerce platform will be very distinct from the training data set needed to create a self-driving car. Nevertheless, in the industrial sectors the core machine learning mechanism stays the same. No wonder, there is a lot of research going on to automate the process of feature engineering.

Evaluation

Essentially, in context of ML "evaluation" is referred to as the method of assessing various hypotheses or models to select one model over another. An "evaluation function" is needed to distinguish between effective classifiers from the vague ones. The evaluation function is also known as the "objective," "utility," or "scoring" function. The machine-learning algorithm has its own internal evaluation function that is usually very different from the researchers ' external evaluation function used to optimize the classifier. Usually, the evaluation function is described as the first phase of the project before selecting the data representation tool. For example, the self-driving car machine learning model has the feature to identify pedestrians in its vicinity at near-zero false-negative and low false-positive rate as an "evaluation function" and the pre-existing condition that needs to be "represented" using applicable data features.

Optimization

The process of searching the hypothesis space of the represented machine learning model to identify the highest-scoring classifier and achieve better evaluation is called "optimization." For algorithms with more than one optimum classifier, selecting the optimization method is very critical in determining the generated classifier and achieving a more effective model of learning. There is a variety of "off-the-shelf optimizers" on the market to kick off new machine learning models before replacing them with custom-designed optimizers.

Machine Learning in Practice

The complete process of machine learning is much more extensive than just the development and application of machine learning algorithms and can be divided into steps below:

1. Define the goals of the project taking into careful consideration all the prior knowledge and domain expertise available. Goals can easily become ambiguous since there are always additional things you want to achieve than practically possible to implement.

2. The data pre-processing and cleaning must result in a high-quality data set. This is the most critical and time-consuming step of the whole project. The larger the volume of data, the more noise it brings to the training data set which must be eradicated before feeding to the learner system.

3. Selection of appropriate learning model to meet the requirements of your project. This process tends to be rather simple given the various types of data models available in the market.

4. Depending on the domain the machine learning model is applied to, the results may or may not require a clear

understanding of the model by human experts as long as the model can successfully deliver desired results.

5. The final step is to consolidate and deploy the knowledge or information gathered from the model to be used on an industrial level.

6. The whole cycle from step 1 to 5 listed above is iteratively repeated until a result that can be used in practice is achieved.

Importance of Machine Learning

The seemingly unstoppable interest in ML stems from the same variables that have made "data mining" and "Bayesian analysis" more common than ever before. The underlying factors contributing to this popularity are increasing quantities and data varieties, cheaper and more effective computational processing, and inexpensive data storage. To get a sense of how significant machine learning is in our everyday lives, it is simpler to state what part of our cutting-edge way of life has not been touched by it. The "smart machines" intended to expand human capacities and improve efficiencies are influencing each aspect of human life. Artificial Intelligence and machine learning technology is the focal precept of the "Fourth Industrial Revolution," that could possibly question our thoughts regarding being "human."

"Google's self-driving cars and robots get a lot of press, but the company's real future is in machine learning, the technology that enables computers to get smarter and more personal."
– Eric Schmidt, Google

All of these factors imply that models that can analyze larger, more complicated data while delivering highly accurate results in a short period can be produced rapidly and automatically on a much larger scale. Companies can easily identify potential growth opportunities or avoid unknown hazards by constructing desired machine learning models that meet their business requirements. Data runs through the vein of every company. Increasingly, data-driven strategies create a distinction between winning or losing the competition. Machine learning offers the magic of unlocking the importance of business and customer data to lead to actionable measures and decisions that can skyrocket a company's business and market share.

Machine learning has demonstrated over recent years that many distinct tasks can be automated which were once deemed as activities only people could carry out, such as image recognition, text processing, and gaming.

In 2014, Machine Learning and AI professionals believed the board game "Go" would take at least ten years for the machine to defeat its greatest player in the world. However, they were proved mistaken by "Google's DeepMind," which showed that machines are capable of learning which moves to take into account even in such a complicated game as "Go." In the world of gaming, machines have seen much more innovations such as "Dota Bot" from the "OpenAI" team. Machine learning is bound to have enormous economic and social impacts on our day-to-day lives. A complete set of work activities and the entire industrial spectrum could potentially be automated, and the labor market will be transformed forever.

"Machine learning is a method of data analysis that automates analytical model building. It is a branch of artificial intelligence based on the idea that systems can learn from data, identify patterns and make decisions with minimal human intervention."

- SAS

Repetitive learning automation and information revelation. Unlike robotic automation driven by hardware that merely automates manual tasks, machine learning continuously and reliably enables the execution of high quantity, high volume and computer-oriented tasks. Artificial intelligence machine learning algorithms help to adapt to the changing landscape by enabling a machine or system to learn, to take note of and reduce its previous mistakes. Machine learning algorithm works as a classifier or a forecasting tool to develop unique abilities and to define data patterns and structure. For instance, an algorithm for machine learning has created a model that will teach itself how to play chess and even how to create product suggestions based on consumer activity and behavioral data. This model is so effective because it can easily adjust to any new data set.

Machine learning allows the assessment of deeper and wider data sets by means of neural networks comprising several hidden layers. Just a couple of years ago, a scheme for detecting fraud with countless hidden layers would have been considered a work of imagination. A completely new world is on the horizon with the emergence of big data and unimaginable computer capabilities. The data on the machines is like the gas on the vehicle; more data addition leads to faster and more accurate results. Deep learning models thrive with a wealth of data because they benefit from the information immediately. The machine-learning algorithms have led to incredible accuracy through the« deep neural networks». Increased accuracy is obtained from deep learning, for instance, from the regular and extensive use of smart technology such as "Amazon Alexa" and "Google Search."

These "deep neural networks" also boost our healthcare sector. Technologies like image classification and the recognition of objects are now able to detect cancer with the same precision as a heavily qualified radiologist on MRIs.

Artificial intelligence enables the use of big data analytics in combination with algorithm for machine learning to be enhanced and improved. Data has developed like its own currency and can readily become "intellectual property" when algorithms are self-learning. The crude information is comparable to a gold mine in that the more and more you dig, the more you can dig out or extract "gold" or meaningful insights. The use of machine learning algorithms for the data allows faster discovery of the appropriate solutions and can make these solutions more useful. Bear in mind that the finest data will always be the winner, even though everyone uses similar techniques.

"Humans can typically create one or two good models a week; machine learning can create thousands of models a week."
- Thomas Davenport, The Wall Street Journal

Machine Learning Algorithms

By utilizing prior computations and underlying algorithms, machines are now capable of learning from and training on their own to generate high quality, readily reproducible decisions and results. The notion of machine learning has been around for a long time now, but the latest advances in machine learning algorithms have made large data processing and analysis feasible for computers. This is achieved by applying sophisticated and complicated mathematical calculations using high speed and frequency automation. Today's advanced computing machines are able to analyze humongous information quantities quickly and deliver quicker and more precise outcomes. Companies using machine learning algorithms have increased flexibility to change the training data set to satisfy their company needs and train the machines accordingly. These tailored algorithms of machine learning enable companies to define potential hazards and possibilities for development. Typically, machine learning algorithms are used in cooperation with artificial intelligence technology and cognitive techniques to create computers extremely efficient and extremely effective in processing large quantities of information or big data and to generate extremely precise outcomes.

There are four fundamental types of machine learning algorithms available today:

Supervised Machine Learning Algorithms

Due to their ability to evaluate and apply the lessons learned from prior iterations and interactions to fresh input data set, the supervised learning algorithms are commonly used in predictive big data analysis. Based on the instructions given to effectively predict and forecast future occurrences, these algorithms can label all their ongoing runs. For instance, people can program the machine as "R" (Run), "N" (Negative) or "P" (Positive) to label its data points. The algorithm for machine learning will then label the input data as programmed and obtain data inputs with the right outputs. The algorithm will compare its own produced output to the "anticipated or correct" output, identifying future changes that can be created and fixing mistakes to make the model more precise and smarter. By using methods such as "regression," "prediction," "classification" and "ingredient boosting" to train the machine learning algorithms well, any new input data can be fed into the machine as a set of "target" data to orchestrate the learning program as desired. This "known training data set" jump-starts the analytical process followed by the learning algorithm to produce an "inferred feature" that can be used to generate forecasts and predictions based on output values for future occurrences. For instance, financial institutions and banks rely strongly on monitoring machine learning algorithms to detect credit card fraud and predict the probability of a prospective credit card client failing to make their credit payments on time.

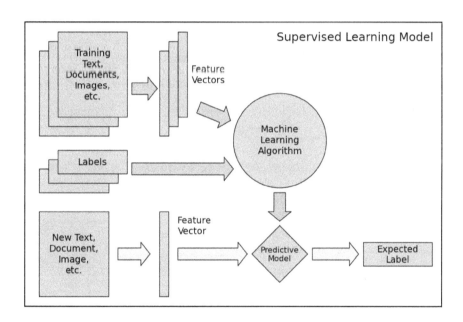

Unsupervised Machine Learning Algorithms

Companies often find themselves in a scenario where information sources are inaccessible that are needed to produce a labeled and classified training data set. Using unsupervised ML algorithms is perfect in these circumstances. Unsupervised ML algorithms are widely used to define how the machine can generate "inferred features" to elucidate a concealed construct from the stack of unlabeled and unclassified data collection. These algorithms can explore the data in order to define a structure within the data mass. Unlike the supervised machine learning algorithms, the unsupervised algorithms fail to identify the correct output, although they are just as effective as the supervised learning algorithms in investigating input data and drawing inferences. These algorithms can be used to identify information outliers, generate tailored and custom product recommendations, classify text subjects using methods such as "self-organizing maps," "singular value decomposition" and "k-means clustering." For instance, customer identification with shared shopping characteristics that can be segmented into particular groups and focused on comparable marketing strategies and campaigns. As a result, in the online marketing world, unsupervised learning algorithms are extremely popular.

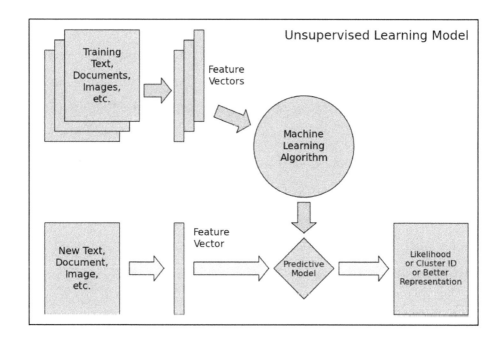

Semi-Supervised Machine Learning Algorithms

Highly versatile, the "semi-supervised machine learning algorithms" are capable of using both labeled and unlabeled information set to learn from and train themselves. These algorithms are a "hybrid" of algorithms that are supervised and unsupervised. Typically, with a small volume of labeled data, the training data set is comprised of predominantly unlabeled data. The use of analytical methods including "forecast," "regression" and "classification" in conjunction with semi-supervised learning algorithms enable the machine to considerably enhance its learning precision and training capabilities. These algorithms are commonly used in instances where it is highly resource-intensive and less cost-effective for the business to generate labeled training data set from raw unlabeled data. Companies use semi-supervised learning algorithms on their systems to avoid incurring extra costs of staff and equipment. For instance, implementation for "facial recognition" technology needs a huge amount of facial data distributed across various sources of input. The raw data pre-processing, processing, classification and labeling, acquired from sources such as internet cameras, needs a lot of resources and thousands of hours of job to be used as a training data set.

Reinforcement Machine Learning Algorithms

The "reinforcement machine learning algorithms" are much more distinctive in that they learn from the environment. These algorithms conduct activities and record the outcomes of each action diligently, which would have been either a failure resulting in mistake or reward for good performance. The two primary features that differentiate the reinforcement learning algorithms are the research method of "trial and error" and feedback loop of "delayed reward." Using a range of calculations, the computer constantly analyzes input data and sends a reinforcement signal for each right or anticipated output to ultimately optimize the end result. The algorithm develops a straightforward action and reward feedback loop to evaluate record and learn which actions have been effective and in a shorter period have resulted in correct or expected output. The use of these algorithms allows the system to automatically determine optimal behaviors and maximize its efficiency within the constraints of a particular context. The reinforcement machine learning algorithms are therefore strongly used in gaming, robotics engineering and navigation systems.

The machine learning algorithms have proliferated to hundreds and thousands and counting. Here are some of the most widely used algorithms:

1. Regression

The "regression" techniques fall under the category of supervised machine learning. They help predict or describe a particular numerical value based on the set of prior information, such as anticipating the cost of a property based on previous cost information for similar characteristics. Regression techniques vary from simple (such as "linear regression") to complex (such as "regular linear regression," "polynomial regression," "decision trees," "random forest regression" and "neural networks," among others).

The simplest method of all is **"linear regression,"** where the line's "mathematical equation (y= m*x+b) is used to model the data collection." Multiple "data pairs (x, y)" can train a "linear regression" model by calculating the position and slope of a line that can decrease the total distance between the data points and the line. In other words, the calculation of the "slope (m)" and "y-intercept (b)" is used for a line that produces the highest approximation for data observations.

For example, using "linear regression" technique to generate predictions for the energy consumption (in kWh) of houses by collecting the age of the house, no. of bedrooms, square footage area and number of installed electronic equipment. Now, we have more than one input (year built, square footage) it is possible to use "linear multi-variable regression." The underlying process is the same as "one-to - one linear regression"; however, the line created was based on the number of variables in multi-dimensional space.

The plot below demonstrates how well the model of linear regression fits the real construction energy consumption. In case where you could gather house characteristics such as year built and square footage, but you do not understand the house's energy consumption then you are better off using the fitted line to generate approximations for the house's energy consumption.

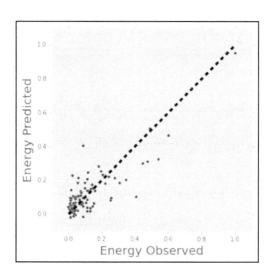

"Multiple Linear Regression" tends to be the most common form of "regression" technique used in data science and the majority of statistical tasks. Just like the "linear regression" technique, there will be an output variable "Y" in "multiple linear regression." However, the distinction now is that we are going to have numerous "X" or independent variables generating predictions for "Y."

For instance, a model developed for predicting the cost of housing in Washington DC will be driven by "multiple linear regression" technique. The cost of housing in Washington DC will be the "Y" or dependent variable for the model. "X" or the independent variables for this model will include data points such as vicinity to public transport, schooling district, square footage, number of rooms, which will eventually determine the market price of the housing.

The mathematical equation for this model can be written as below:

$$\textit{``housing\_price} = \beta_0 + \beta_1 \, \textit{sq\_foot} + \beta_2 \, \textit{dist\_transport} + \beta_3$$
$$\textit{num\_rooms''}$$

"Polynomial regression" - Our models developed a straight line in the last two types of "regression" techniques. This straight line is a result of the connection between "X" and "Y" which is "linear" and does not alter the influence "X" has on "Y" as the changing values of "X." Our model will lead in a row with a curve in "polynomial regression."

If we attempted to fit a graph with non-linear features using "linear regression," it would not yield the best fit line for the non-linear features. For instance, the graph on the left shown in the picture below has the scatter plot depicting an upward trend, but with a curve. A straight line does not operate in this situation. Instead, we will generate a line with a curve to match the curve in our data with a polynomial regression, like the chart on the right shown in the picture below. The equation of a polynomial will appear like the linear equation, the distinction being that one or more of the "X" variables will be linked to some polynomial expression. For instance,

$$\textbf{``Y = mX}^2\textbf{+b''}$$

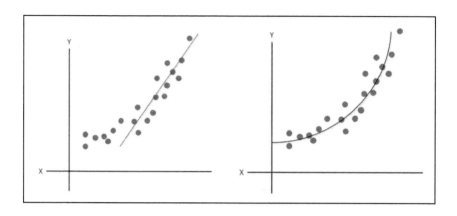

Another technique of reduction is called **"LASSO regression."**
A very complementary technique to the "ridge regression," "lasso
regression" promotes the use of simpler and leaner models to
generate predictions. In lasso regression, the model reduces the
value of coefficients relatively more rigidly. LASSO stands for the
"least absolute shrinkage and selection operator." Data on our
scatterplot, like the mean or median values of the data
are reduced to a more compact level. We use this when the model
is experiencing high multicollinearity similar to the "ridge
regression" model.

A hybrid of "LASSO" and "ridge regression" methods is known as
"ElasticNet Regression." Its primary objective is to
further enhance the accuracy of the predictions generated by the
"LASSO regression" technique. "ElasticNet Regression" is a
confluence of both "LASSO" and "ridge regression" techniques of

rewarding smaller coefficient values. All three of these designs are available in the R and Python "Glmnet suite."

"Bayesian regression" models are useful when there is a lack of sufficient data or available data has poor distribution. These regression models are developed based on probability distributions rather than data points, meaning the resulting chart will appear as a bell curve depicting the variance with the most frequently occurring values in the center of the curve. The dependent variable "Y" in "Bayesian regression" is not a valuation but a probability. Instead of predicting a value, we try to estimate the probability of an occurrence. This is regarded as "frequentist statistics," and this sort of statistics is built on the "Bayes theorem." "Frequentist statistics" hypothesize if an event is going to occur and the probability of it occurring again in the future.

"Conditional probability" is integral to the concept of "frequentist statistics." Conditional probability pertains to the events whose results are dependent on one another. Events can also be conditional, which means the preceding event can potentially alter the probability of the next event. Assume you have a box of M&Ms, and you want to understand the probability of withdrawing distinct colors of the M&Ms from the bag. If you have a set of three yellow M&Ms and three blue M&Ms and on your first draw you get a blue M&M, and then with your next draw from the box the probability of taking out a blue M&M will be lower than the first draw. This is a classic example of "conditional probability." On the other hand, an independent event is the flipping of a coin, meaning the preceding coin flip does not alter the probability of the next flip of the coin. Therefore, a coin flip is not an example of "conditional probability."

2. Classification

The method of "classification" is another class of "supervised machine learning," which can generate predictions or explanations for a "class value." For example, this method can be used to predict the if an online customer will actually purchase a particular product. The result generated will be reported as a yes or no response i.e. "buyer" or "not a buyer." However, techniques of classification are not restricted to two classes. A classification technique, for instance, could assist to evaluate whether a specified picture includes a sedan or an SUV. The output will be three different values in this case: 1) the picture contains a sedan, 2) the picture contains an SUV, or 3) the picture does not contain either a sedan or an SUV.

"Logistic regression" is considered the easiest classification algorithm, though the term comes across as a "regression" technique, but that is far from the reality. "Logistic regression" generates estimations for the likelihood of an event taking place based on single or multiple input values. For example, to generate estimation for the likelihood of a student being accepted to a specific university, a "logistic regression" will use the standardized testing scores and university testing scores for a student as inputs. The generated prediction is a probability, ranging between '0' and '1,' where 1 is full assurance. For the student, if the estimated likelihood is greater than 0.5, then the prediction would be that they will be accepted. If the projected probability were less than 0.5, the prediction would be that they would be denied admission.

The following graph shows the ratings of past learners as well as whether they have been accepted. Logistic regression enables the creation of a line that can represent the "decision boundary."

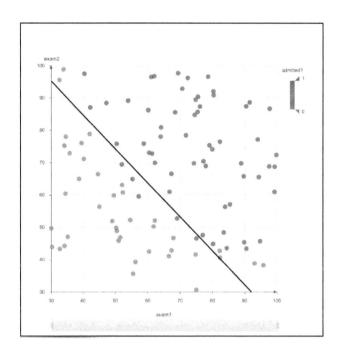

3. Clustering

We enter the category of unsupervised machine learning, with "clustering methods" because its objective is to "group or cluster observations with comparable features." Clustering methods do not use output data to train but allow the output to be defined by the algorithm. Only data visualizations can be used in clustering techniques to check the solution's quality.

"K-Means clustering," where 'K' is used to represent the number of "clusters" that the customer elects to generate and is the most common clustering method. (Note that different methods for selecting K value, such as the "elbow technique," are available.)

Steps used by K-Means clustering to process the data points:

1. The data centers are selected randomly by 'K.'
2. Assigns each data point to the nearest centers that have been randomly generated.
3. Re-calculates each cluster's center.
4. If centers do not change (or have minor change), the process will be completed.
   - Otherwise, we will go back to step two. (Set a maximum amount of iterations in advance to avoid being stuck in an infinite loop, if the center of the cluster continues to alter.)

The following plot applies "K-Means" to a building data set. Each column in the plot shows each building's efficiency. The four measurements relate to air conditioning, heating, installed electronic appliances (refrigerators, TV) and cooking gas. For simplicity of interpretation of the results, 'K' can be set to value '2' for clustering, wherein one cluster will be selected as an efficient building group and the other cluster as an inefficient building group. You see the place of the structures on the left as well as a couple of the building characteristics used as inputs on the right: installed electronic appliances and heating.

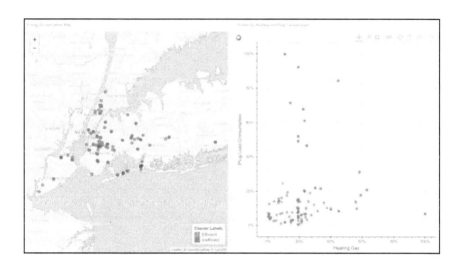

4. Dimension Reduction

As the name indicates, to extract the least significant information (sometimes redundant columns) from a data set, we use "dimensionality reduction." In practice, data sets tend to contain hundreds or even thousands of rows (also known as characteristics), which makes it essential to reduce the total number of rows. For example, pictures may contain thousands of pixels; not all those pixels are important for the analysis. Alternatively, a large number of measurements or experiments can be applied to every single chip while testing microchips within the manufacturing process, the majority of which produce redundant data. In such scenarios, "dimensionality reduction" algorithms are leveraged to manage the data set.

Principal Component Analysis

"Principal Component Analysis" or (PCA) is the most common "dimension reduction technique," which decreases the size of the "feature space" by discovering new vectors that are capable of maximizing the linear variety of the data. When the linear correlations of the data are powerful, PCA can dramatically decrease the data dimension without losing too much information. PCA is one of the fundamental algorithms of machine learning. It enables you to decrease the data dimension, losing as little information as possible. It is used in many fields such as object recognition, vision of computers, compression of information, etc. The calculation of the main parts is limited to the calculation of the initial data's own vectors and covariance matrix values or to the data matrix's unique decomposition. Through one, we can convey several indications, merge, so to speak, and operate with a simpler model already. Of course, most probably, data loss will not be avoided, but the PCA technique will assist us to minimize any losses.

T-Stochastic Neighbor Embedding (t-SNE)

Another common technique is "t-Stochastic Neighbor Embedding (t-SNE)," which results in decrease of non-linear dimensionality. This technique is primarily used for data visualization, with potential use for machine learning functions such as space reduction and clustering.

The next plot demonstrates "MNIST database" analysis of handwritten digits. "MNIST" includes a large number of digit pictures from 0 to 9, used by scientists to test "clustering" and "classification" algorithms. Individual row of the data set represents "vectorized version" of the original picture (size 28x28 = 784 pixels) and a label (0, 1, 2 and so on) for each picture. Note that the dimensionality is therefore reduced from 784 pixels to 2-D in the plot below. Two-dimensional projecting enables visualization of the initial high-dimensional data set.

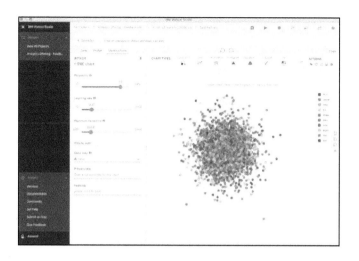

5. Ensemble Methods

Think that you have chosen to construct a car because you are not pleased with the variety of cars available in the market and online. You may start by discovering the best option for every component that you need. The resulting car will outshine all the other alternatives with the assembly of all these excellent components.

"Ensemble methods" use the same concept of mixing several predictive models (controlled machine learning) to obtain results of greater quality than any of the models can generate on their own. The "Random Forest" algorithms, for instance, is an "ensemble method" that collates various trained "Decision Trees" with different data set samples. Consequently, the quality of predictions generated by "Random Forest" method is better than the quality of the estimated predictions generated by only one "Decision Tree."

Think of "ensemble methods" as an approach for reducing a single machine learning model's variance and bias. This is essential because under certain circumstances, any specified model may be accurate but completely incorrect under other circumstances. The relative accuracy could be overturned with another model. The quality of the predictions is balanced by merging the two models.

6. Transfer Learning

Imagine you are a data scientist focusing on the clothing industry. You have been training a high-quality learning model for months to be able to classify pictures of "women's tops" as tops, tank tops and blouses. You have been tasked to create a comparable model for classification of pants pictures such as jeans, trousers and chinos. With the use of "Transfer Learning" method, the understanding incorporated into the first model be seamlessly transferred and applied to the second model.

Transfer Learning pertains to the re-use and adaptation of a portion of a previously trained neural network to a fresh but comparable assignment. Specifically, once a neural network has been successfully trained for a particular task, a proportion of the trained layers can be easily transferred and combined with new layers that are then trained on pertinent data for the new task. This new "neural network" can learn and adapt rapidly to the new assignment by incorporating a few layers.

The primary benefit of transferring learning is decrease in the volume of data required to train the neural network resulting in cost savings for the development of "deep learning algorithms." Not to forget how hard it can be to even procure a sufficient amount of labeled data to train the model.

Suppose in this example, you are using a neural network with 20 hidden layers for the "women's top" model. You understand after running a few tests that 16 of the women's top model layers can be transferred and combined them with a new set of data to train on pants pictures. Therefore, the new pants model will have 17 concealed layers. The input and output of both the tasks are distinct, but the reusable layers are capable of summarizing the data appropriate to both, e.g. clothing, zippers, and shape of the garment.

Transfer learning is getting increasingly popular, so much so that for basic "deep learning tasks" such as picture and text classification, a variety of high quality pre trained models are already available in the market.

7. Natural Language Processing

A majority of the knowledge and information pertaining to our world is in some type of human language. Once deemed as impossible to achieve, today computers are capable of reading large volumes of books and blogs within minutes. Although, computers are still unable to fully comprehend "human text," but they can be trained to perform specific tasks. Mobile devices, for instance, can be trained to auto-complete text messages or fix spelling mistakes. Machines have been trained enough to hold straightforward conversations like humans.

"Natural Language Processing" (NLP) is not exactly a method of ML; instead it is a commonly used technique to produce texts for machine learning. Consider multitude of formats of tons of text files (words, internet blogs etc.). Most of these text files are usually flooded with typing errors, grammatically incorrect characters and phrases that need to be filtered out. The most popular text processing model available in the market today do "Stanford University" researchers develop "NLTK (Natural Language ToolKit).

The easiest approach to map texts into numerical representations is calculation of the frequency of each word contained in every text document. For example, an integer matrix where individual rows represent one text document and every column represents a single word. This word frequency representation matrix is frequently referred to as the "Term Frequency Matrix" (TFM).

From there, individual matrix entries can be separated by a weight of how essential every single term is within the whole stack of papers. This form of matrix representation of a text document is called "Term Frequency Inverse Document Frequency" (TFIDF), which usually yields better performance for machine learning tasks.

8. Word Embedding

"Term Frequency Matrix" and "Term Frequency Inverse Document Frequency" are numerical representations of text papers that only take into account frequency and weighted frequencies to represent text files. On the other hand, "Word Embedding" in a document is capable of capturing the actual context of a word. Embedding can quantify the similarity between phrases within the context of the word, which subsequently allows the execution of arithmetic operations with words.

"Word2Vec" is a neural network-based technique that can map phrases to a numerical vector in a corpus. These vectors are then used to discover synonyms, do arithmetic with words or phrases, or to represent text files. Let us suppose, for instance, a large enough body of text files was used to estimate word embedding. Suppose the words "king, queen, man and female" are found in the corpus and vector ("word") is the number vector representing the word "word." We can conduct arithmetic procedure with numbers to estimate vector('woman'):

vector('king') + *vector('woman') − vector('man')* ~ *vector('queen')*

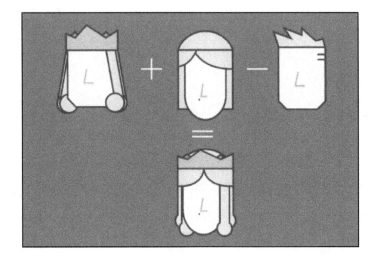

Word depictions enable similarities to be found between phrases by calculating the "cosine similarity" between the vector representations of the two words. The "cosine similarity" gives a measure of the angle between two vectors.

We use machine learning techniques to calculate word embedding, but this is often a preliminary step in implementing a machine learning algorithm on top of the word embedding method. For example, the "Twitter" user database containing large volume of "tweets" can be leveraged to understand which of these customers purchased a house recently. We can merge "Word2Vec" with a logistic regression to generate predictions on the likelihood of a new "Twitter" user purchasing a home.

9. Decision Trees

To refresh your memory; a machine learning decision tree can be defined as "a tree like graphical representation of the decision-making process, by taking into consideration all the conditions or factors that can influence the decision and the consequences of those decisions." Decision trees are considered one of the simplest "supervised machine learning algorithms," with three main elements: "branch nodes" representing conditions of the data set, "edges" representing ongoing decision process and "leaf nodes" representing end of the decision.

The two types of decision trees are "Classification tree" that is used to classify Data based on the existing data available in the system; "Regression tree" which is used to make forecast for predictions for future events based on the existing data in the system. Both of these trees are heavily used in machine learning algorithms. A widely used terminology for decision trees is "Classification and Regression trees" or "CART."

Let us look at how you can build a simple decision tree based on a real-life example.

Step 1: Identify what decision needs to be made, which will serve as a "root node" for the decision tree. For this example, decision needs to be made on "What would you like to do over the weekend?" Unlike real trees, decision tree has its roots on top instead of the bottom.

Step 2: Identify conditions or influencing factors for your decision, which will serve as "branch nodes" for the decision tree. For this example, conditions could include "would you like to spend the weekend alone or with your friends?" and "how is the weather going to be?"

Step 3: As you answer the conditional questions, you may run into additional conditions that you might have ignored. You will now continue to your final decision by processing all the conditional questions individually, these bifurcations will serve as "edges" of your decision tree.

Step 4: Once you have processed all of the permutations and combinations and eventually made your final decision that final decision will serve as the "leaf node" of your decision tree. Unlike "branch nodes," there are no further bifurcations possible from a "leaf node."

Here is the graphical representation of your decision for the example above:

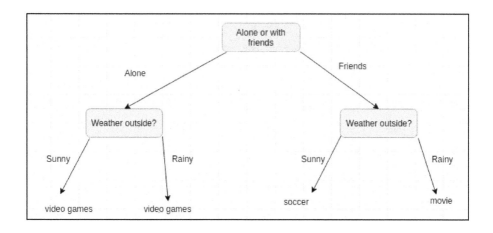

As you would expect from a decision tree, you have obtained a "model representing a set of sequential and hierarchical decisions that ultimately lead to some final decision." This example is at a very high-level to help you develop an understanding of the concept of decision trees. The data science and machine learning decision trees are much more complicated and bigger with hundreds and thousands of branch nodes and edges.

10.   Apriori machine learning algorithm

"Apriori algorithm" is another unsupervised ML algorithm that can produce rules of association from a specified set of data. "Association rule" simply means if an item X exists then the item Y has a predefined probability of existence. Most rules of association are produced in the format of "IF-THEN" statements. For instance, "IF" someone purchases an iPhone, "THEN" they have most likely purchased an iPhone case as well. The Apriori algorithm is able to draw these findings by initially observing the

83

number of individuals who purchased an iPhone case while making an iPhone purchase and generating a ratio obtained by dividing the number individuals who bought a new iPhone (1000) with individuals who also bought an iPhone case (800) with their new iPhones.

The fundamental principles of Apriori ML Algorithm are:

- If a set of events have high frequency of occurrence, then all subsets of that event set will also have high frequency of occurrence.
- If a set of events occur occasionally, then all supersets of the event set of will occur occasionally as well.

Apriori algorithm has wide applicability in following areas:

"Detecting Adverse Drug Reactions"

"Apriori algorithm" is used to analyze healthcare data such as the drugs administered to the patient, characteristics of each patient, harmful side effects experienced by the patient, the original diagnosis, among others. This analysis generates rules of association that provide insight on the characteristic of the patient and the administered drug that potentially contributed to adverse side effects of the drug.

"Market Basket Analysis"

Some of the leading online e-commerce businesses including "Amazon," use Apriori algorithm to gather insights on products that have high likelihood of being bought together and products that can have an upsell with product promotions and discount offers. For instance, a retailer to generate prediction such as could use Apriori: customers purchasing sugar and flour have high likelihood of purchasing eggs to bake cookies and cakes.

"Auto-Complete Applications"

The highly cherished auto-complete feature on "Google" is another common Apriori application. When the user starts typing in their keywords for a search, the search engine searches its database, for other related phrases that are usually typed in after a particular word.

11. Support vector machine learning algorithm

"Support Vector Machine" or (SVM) is a type of "supervised ML algorithm," used for "classification" or "regression," where the data set trains SVM on "classes" in order to be able to classify new inputs. This algorithm operates by classifying the data into various "classes" by discovering a line (hyper-plane) that divides the collection of training data into "classes." Due to availability of various linear hyper-planes, this algorithm attempts to maximize the distance between the different "classes" involved, which is called "margin maximization." By identifying the line that maximizes the class distance, the likelihood of generalizing apparent to unseen data can be improved.

SVM's can be categorized into two as follows:

- "Linear SVM's" – The training data or classifiers can be divided by a hyper-plane.

- "Non-Linear SVM's" – Unlike linear SVMs, in "non-linear SVM's" the possibility to separate the training data with a hyper-plane is nonexistent. For example, the Face Detection training data consists of a group of facial images and another group of non-facial images. The training data is so complicated under such circumstances, that it is difficult to obtain a feature representation of every single vector. It is extremely complex to separate the facial data set linearly from the non-facial data set.

SVM is widely used by different economic organizations for stock market forecasting. For example, SVM is leveraged to compare relative stock performances of various stocks in the same industrial sector. The classifications generated by SVM, aids in the investment related decision-making process.

Chapter 3: Introduction to Python Coding

Python was first implemented in 1989 and is regarded as highly user-friendly and simple to learn programming language for entry level coders and amateurs. It is a high-level programming language, commonly used for general purposes. It was originally developed by Guido van Rossum at the "Center Wickenden & Informatica (CWI), Netherlands," in 1980s and introduced by the "Python Software Foundation" in 1991. It was designed primarily to emphasize readability of programming code, and its syntax enables programmers to convey ideas using fewer lines of code. Python programming language increases the speed of operation while allowing for higher efficiency in creating system integrations. It is regarded ideal for individuals newly interested in programming or coding and need to comprehend programming fundamentals. This stems from the fact that Python reads almost the same as English language. Therefore, it requires less time to understand how the language works and focus can be directed in learning the basics of programming.

Python is an interpreted language that supports automatic memory management and object-oriented programming. This extremely intuitive and flexible programming language can be used for coding projects such as machine learning algorithms, web applications, data mining and visualization, game development.

Installation Instructions for Python

Follow the s instructions below to download and install Python on your operating system by referring to the relevant section. The latest version of Python released in the middle of the 2019 is Python 3.8.0. Make sure to download and install the most recent and stable version of Python at the time.

WINDOWS

1. From the official Python website, click on the "Downloads" icon and select Windows.

2. Click on the "Download Python 3.8.0" button to view all the downloadable files.

3. On subsequent screen, select the Python version you would like to download. In this book, we will be using the Python 3 version under "Stable Releases." So, scroll down the page and click on the "Download Windows x86-64 executable installer" link as shown in the picture below.

- Python 3.8.0 - Oct. 14, 2019

Note that Python 3.8.0 *cannot* be used on Windows XP or earlier.

- Download Windows help file
- Download Windows x86-64 embeddable zip file
- Download Windows x86-64 executable installer
- Download Windows x86-64 web-based installer
- Download Windows x86 embeddable zip file
- Download Windows x86 executable installer
- Download Windows x86 web-based installer

4. A pop-up window titled "python-3.8.0-amd64.exe" will be shown.

5. Click on the "Save File" button to start downloading the file.

6. Once the download has completed, double click the saved file icon and a "Python 3.8.0 (64-bit) Setup" pop window will be shown.

7. Make sure that you select the "Install Launcher for all users (recommended)" and the "Add Python 3.8 to PATH" checkboxes. Note – If you already have an older version of Python installed on your system, the "Upgrade Now" button will appear instead of the "Install Now" button and neither of the checkboxes will be shown.

8. Click on "Install Now" and a "User Account Control" pop up window will be shown.

9. A notification stating, "Do you want to allow this app to make changes to your device" will be shown, click on Yes.

10. A new pop up window titled "Python 3.8.0 (64-bit) Setup" will be shown containing a set up progress bar.

11. Once the installation has been completed, a "Set was successful" message will be shown. Click on Close.

12. To verify the installation, navigate to the directory where you installed Python and double click on the python.exe file.

MACINTOSH

1. From the official Python website, click on the "Downloads" icon and select Mac.

2. Click on the "Download Python 3.8.0" button to view all the downloadable files.

3. On subsequent screen, select the Python version you would like to download. In this book, we will be using the Python 3 version under "Stable Releases." So, scroll down the page and click on the "Download macOS 64-bit installer" link under Python 3.8.0, as shown in the picture below.

- Python 3.7.5 - Oct. 15, 2019
  - Download macOS 64-bit/32-bit installer
  - Download macOS 64-bit installer
- Python 3.8.0 - Oct. 14, 2019
  - Download macOS 64-bit installer
- Python 3.7.4 - July 8, 2019
  - Download macOS 64-bit/32-bit installer
  - Download macOS 64-bit installer
- Python 3.6.9 - July 2, 2019

4. A pop-up window titled "python-3.8.0-macosx10.9.pkg" will be shown.

5. Click "Save File" to start downloading the file.

6. Once the download has completed, double click the saved file icon and an "Install Python" pop window will be shown.

7. Click "Continue" to proceed and the terms and conditions pop up window will appear.

8. Click Agree and then click "Install."

9. A notification requesting administrator permission and password will be shown. Enter your system password to start installation.

10. Once the installation has finished, an "Installation was successful" message will appear. Click on the Close button and you are all set.

11. To verify the installation, navigate to the directory where you installed Python and double click on the python launcher icon that will take you to the Python Terminal.

LINUX

- **For Red Hat, CentOS or Fedora**, install the python3 and python3-devel packages.
- **For Debian or Ubuntu**, install the python3.x and python3.x-dev packages.
- **For Gentoo**, install the '=python-3.x*' ebuild (you may have to unmask it first).

1. From the official Python website, click on the "Downloads" icon and select Linux/UNIX.
2. Click on the "Download Python 3.8.0" button to view all the downloadable files.
3. On subsequent screen, select the Python version you would like to download. In this book, we will be using the Python 3 version under "Stable Releases." So, scroll down the page and click on the "Download Gzipped source tarball" link under Python 3.8.0, as shown in the picture below.

- Download Gzipped source tarball
- Download XZ compressed source tarball
  - Python 3.8.0 - Oct. 14, 2019
    - Download Gzipped source tarball
    - Download XZ compressed source tarball
  - Python 3.7.4 - July 8, 2019
    - Download Gzipped source tarball
    - Download XZ compressed source tarball

4. A pop-up window titled "python-3.7.5.tgz" will be shown.
5 Click "Save File" to begin downloading the file.
6. Once the download has finished, double click the saved file icon and an "Install Python" pop window will appear.
7. Follow the prompts on the screen to complete the installation process.

Getting Started

With the Python terminal installed on your computer, you can now start writing and executing the Python code. All Python codes are written in a text editor as (.py) files and executed on the Python interpreter command line as shown in the code below, where "nineplanets.py" is the name of the Python file:

"C: \Users\Your Name\python nineplanets.py"

You will be able to test a small code without writing it in a file and simply executing it as a command line itself by typing the code below on the Mac, Windows or Linux command line, as shown below:

"C: \Users\Your Name\python"

In case the command above does not work, use the code below instead:

"C: \Users\Your Name\py"

Indentation – The importance of indentation, which is the number of spaces preceding the code, is fundamental to the Python coding structure. In most programming languages indentation is added to enhance the readability of the code. However, in Python the indentation is used to indicate execution of a subset of the code, as shown in the code below

If 7 > 2:
        print ('Seven is greater than two')

Indentation precedes the second line of code with the print command. If the indentation is skipped and the code was written as below, an error will be triggered:

If 7 > 2:
print ('Seven is greater than two')

The number of spaces can be modified but is required to have at least one space. For example, you can execute the code below with higher indentation but for a specific set of code same number of spaces must be used or you will receive an error.

If 7 > 2:
   print ('Seven is greater than two')

Adding Comments – In Python comments can be added to the code by starting the code comment lines with a "#," as shown in the example below:

#Any relevant comments will be added here
print ('Nine planets')

Comments serve as a description of the code and will not executed by the Python terminal. Make sure to remember that any comments at the end of code line will lead to the entire code line being skipped by the Python terminal as shown in the code below. Comments can be very useful in case you need to stop the execution when you are testing the code.

print ('Nine Planets')   *#Comments added here*

Multiple lines of comments can be added by starting each code line with "#," as shown below:

#Comments added here
#Supplementing the comments here
#Further adding the comments here
print ('Nine Planets')

Python Variables

In Python, variables are primarily utilized to save data values without executing a command for it. A variable can be created by simply assigning desired value to it, as shown in the example below:

A = 999
B = 'Patricia'
print (A)
print (B)

A variable could be declared without a specific data type. The data type of a variable can also be modified after its initial declaration, as shown in the example below:

A = 999 # A has data type set as int
A = 'Patricia' # A now has data type str
print (A)

Some of the rules applied to the Python variable names are as follows:

1. Variable names could be as short as single alphabets or more descriptive words like height, weight and more.

2. Variable names could only be started with an underscore character or a letter.

3. Variable names must not start with numbers.

4. Variable names can contain underscores or alphanumeric characters. No other special characters are allowed.

5. Variable names are case sensitive. For example, 'weight,' 'Weight' and 'WEIGHT' will be accounted as three separate variables.

Assigning Value to Variables

In Python, multiple variables can be assigned DISTINCT values in a single code line, as shown in the example below:

A, B, C = 'violet,' maroon, 'teal'
print (A)
print (B)
print (C)

OR multiple variables can be assigned SAME value in a single code line, as shown in the example below:

A, B, C = 'violet'
print (A)
print (B)
print (C)

Python Data Types

Python supports a variety of data types as listed below. To build a solid understanding of the concept of variables you must learn all the Python data types.

Category	Data Type	Example Syntax
Text	*"str"*	'Nine Planets' "Nine Planets" """"Nine Planets""""
Boolean	*"bool"*	'True' 'False'
Mapping (mixed data types, associative array of key and value pairs)	*"dict"*	'{'key8' : 8.0, 5 : True}'
Sequence (may contain mixed data types)	*"list"*	'[8.0, 'character,' True]'
	"tuple"	'[8.0, 'character,' True]'
	"range"	'range (11, 51)' 'range (110, 51, 11, -11, -51, -110)'

Binary	*"bytes"*	b 'byte sequences' b 'byte sequences' bytes ([121, 91, 75, 110])
	"bytearray"	bytearray (b 'byte sequences') bytearray (b 'byte sequences') bytearray ([121, 91. 75, 110])
	"memoryview"	
Set (unordered, no duplicates, mixed data types)	*"set"*	'[8.0, 'character,' True]'
	"frozenset"	'frozenset ([8.0, 'character,' True])'
Numeric	*"int"*	'35'
	"float"	'155e3'
	"complex"	'155 + 2.1j'
Ellipsis (index in NumPy arrays)	*"ellipsis"*	'...' 'Ellipsis'

To view the data type of any object, you can use the *"type ()"* function as shown in the example below:

A = 'Violet'

print (type (A))

Assigning the Data Type to Variables

A new variable can be created by simply declaring a value for it. This set data value will in turn assign the data type to the variable.

To assign a specific data type to a variable, the constructor functions listed below are used:

Constructor Functions	Data Type
A = str ('Nine Planets)'	str
A = int (55)	Int (Must be a whole number, positive or negative with no decimals, no length restrictions)
A = float (14e6)	Float (Floating point number must be positive or negative number with one or more decimals; maybe scientific number an 'e' to specify an exponential power of 10)
A = complex (92j)	Complex (Must be written with a 'j' as an imaginary character)
A = list (('teal,' maroon, 'jade'))	list
A = range (3, 110)	range
A = tuple (('teal,' maroon, 'jade'))	tuple
A = set (('teal,' maroon, 'jade'))	set
A = frozenset (('teal,' 'jade,' maroon))	frozenset

A = dict ('color': maroon, 'year': 1988)	dict
A = bool (False)	bool
A = bytes (542)	bytes
A = bytearray (9)	bytearray
A = memoryview (bytes (525))	memoryview

Python Numbers

In Python programming, you will be working with three different numeric data types, namely, "int," "float" and "complex." In the previous chapter, you learnt the details of what these data types entail but below are some examples to refresh your memory.

Data Type	Example
Int (Must be a whole number, positive or negative with no decimals, no length restrictions)	*388 or 3.42*
Float (Floating point number must be positive or negative number with one or more decimals; maybe scientific number an "e" to specify an exponential power of 10)	*41e4*
Complex (Must be written with a "j" as an imaginary character)	*46j*

Converting One Numeric Data Type to Another

As all Python variables are dynamic in nature, you will be able to convert the data type of these variables if needed by deriving a new variable from the variable that you would like to assign a new data type.

Let us continue building on the exercise discussed above.

```
a = 4.25      # int
b = 7e3       # float
c = -49j      # complex

#conversion from int to float
x = float (a)

#conversion from float to complex
y = complex (b)

#conversion from complex to int
z = float (c)

#conversion from int to complex
x1 = int (a)

print (x)
print (y)
print (z)
print (x1)

print (type (x))
print (type (y))
```

print (type (z))

print (type (x1))

Variable Casting with Constructor Functions

In the discussion and exercise above, you learnt that variables can be declared by simply assigning desired data value to them and thereby the variables will assume the pertinent data type based on the data value. However, Python allows you to specify the data types for variables by using classes or "constructor functions" to define the data type for variables. This process is called "Casting."

Here are the three constructor functions used for "casting" numeric data type to a variable.

Constructor Functions	Data Type
int ()	Will construct an integer number from an integer literal, a string literal (provided the string is representing a whole number) or a float literal (by rounding down to the preceding whole number)
float ()	Will construct a float number from a string literal (provided the string is

	representing a float or an integer), a float literal or an integer literal
complex ()	Will construct a string from a large number of data types, such as integer literals, float literals and strings

Python Strings

In Python, string data type for a variable is denoted by using single, double or triple quotation marks. This implies that you can assign string data value to variable by quoting the string of characters. For example, "welcome" is the same as 'welcome' and "'welcome'."

String Arrays

In Python, string data values are arrays of bytes that represent Unicode characters as true for most programming languages. However, unlike other programming languages, Python lacks data type for individual characters, which are denoted as string data type with length of 1.

The first character of every string is given the position of '0' and subsequently the subsequent characters will have the position as 1, 2, 3 and so on. In order to display desired characters from a string data value, you can use the position of the character enclosed in square brackets. For example, if you wanted to display the fourth character of the string data value "cranberry" of variable "x." You will use the command "print (x [3])"

Slicing

If you would like to view a range of characters, you can do so by specifying the start and the end index of the desired positions and separating the indexes by a colon. For example, to view characters of a string from position 2 to position 5, your code will be *"print (variable [2:5])."*

You can even view the characters starting from the end of the string by using "negative indexes" and start slicing the string from the end of the string. For example, to view characters of a string from position 3 to position 1, your code will be *"print (variable [-3: -2])."*

In order to view the length of the string, you can use the "len ()" function. For example, to view the length of a string, your code will be *"print (len (variable))."*

Python Booleans

In the process of developing a software program, there is often a need to confirm and verify whether an expression is true or false. This is where Python Boolean data type and data values are used. In Python, comparison and evaluation of two data values will result in one of the two Boolean values: "True" or "False."

Here are some examples of comparison statement of numeric data leading to Boolean value:

print (110 > 94)

OUTPUT – True

print (110 > 94)

OUTPUT – False

print (110 > 94)

OUTPUT – False

Let's look at the *"bool ()"* function now, which allows for evaluation of numeric data as well as string data resulting in "True" or "False" Boolean values.

print (bool (93))

OUTPUT - True

print (bool ("Welcome"))

OUTPUT - True

Here are some key points to remember for Booleans:

1. If a statement has some kind of content, it would be evaluated as "True."
2. All string data values will be resulting as "True" unless the string is empty.
3. All numeric values will be resulting as "True" except "0"
4. Lists, Tuples, Set and Dictionaries will be resulting as "True," unless they are empty.
5. Mostly empty values like (), [], {}, "," False, None and 0 will be resulting as "False."
6. Any object created with the "_len_" function that result in the data value as "0" or "False" will be evaluated as "False."

In Python there are various built in functions function that can be evaluated as Boolean, for example, the "isinstance()" function which allows you to determine the data type of an object.

Therefore, in order to check if an object is integer, the code will be as below:

```
X = 10
print (isinstance (X, int))
```

Python Lists

In Python, Lists are collections of data types that can be changed, organized and include duplicate values. Lists are written within square brackets, as shown in the syntax below.

X = ["string1," "string2," "string3"]
print (X)

The same concept of position applies to Lists as the string data type, which dictates that the first string is considered to be at position 0. Subsequently the strings that will follow are given position 1, 2 and so on. You can selectively display desired string from a List by referencing the position of that string inside square bracket in the print command as shown below.

X = ["string1," "string2," "string3"]
print (X [2])

OUTPUT – [string3]

Similarly, the concept of **negative indexing** is also applied to Python List. Let us look at the example below:

X = ["string1," "string2," "string3"]
print (X [-2])

OUTPUT – [string2]

You will also be able to specify a **range of indexes** by indicating the start and end of a range. The result in values of such command on a Python List would be a new List containing only the indicated items. Here is an example for your reference.

X = ["string1," "string2," "string3," "string4," "string5," "string6"]
print (X [3 : 5])

OUTPUT – ["string4," "string5"]

* Remember the first item is at position 0 and the final position of the range (4) is not included.

Now, if you do not indicate the start of this range it will default to the position 0 as shown in the example below:

X = ["string1," "string2," "string3," "string4," "string5," "string6"]
print (X [: 4])

OUTPUT – ["string1," "string2," "string3" , *"string4"*]

Similarly, if you do not indicate the end of this range it will display all the items of the List from the indicated start range to the end of the List, as shown in the example below:

X = ["string1," "string2," "string3," "string4," "string5," "string6"]
print (X [4 :])

OUTPUT – ["string5," "string6"]

You can also specify a **range of negative indexes** to Python Lists, as shown in the example below:

X = ["string1," "string2," "string3," "string4," "string5," "string6"]
print (X [-4 : -1])

OUTPUT – ["string3," "*string4,*" "string5"]

* Remember the last item is at position -1 and the final position of this range (-1) is not included in the Output.

There might be instances when you need to **change the data value** for a Python List. This can be accomplished by referring to the index number of that item and declaring the new value. Let us look at the example below:

X = *["string1," "string2," "string3," "string4," "string5,"*
"string6"]
X [2] = "newstring"
print (X)

OUTPUT – ["string1," "string2," "newstring," "string4," "string5,"
"string6"]

You can also determine the **length** of a Python List using the "len()" function, as shown in the example below:

X = ["string1," "string2," "string3," "string4," "string5"]
print (len (X))

OUTPUT – 5

Python Lists can also be changed by **adding new items** to an existing List using the built-in "append ()" method, as shown in the example below:

X = ["string1," "string2," "string3," "string4," "string5"]
X.append ("newstring")
print (X)

OUTPUT – ["string1," "string2," "string3," "string4," "string5," "newstring"]

You can also, add a new item to an existing Python List at a specific position using the built-in "insert ()" method, as shown in the example below:

X = ["string1," "string2," "string3," "string4"]
X.insert (3, "newstring")
print (X)

OUTPUT – ["string1," "string2," "string3," "newstring"]

There might be instances when you need to **copy** an existing Python List. This can be accomplished by using the built-in "copy ( )" method or the "list ( )" method, as shown in the example below:

X = ["string1," "string2," "string3," "string4," "string5," "string6"]
Y = X.copy( )
print (Y)

OUTPUT – ["string1," "string2," "string3," "string4," "string5," "string6"]

X = ["string1," "string2," "string3," "string4," "string5,"
"string6"]
Y = list (X)
print (Y)

OUTPUT – ["string1," "string2," "string3," "string4," "string5,"
"string6"]

There are multiple built-in methods to **delete items** from a
Python List.

- To selectively delete a specific item, the "remove ()"
  method can be used.
  X = ["string1," "string2," "string3," "string4"]
  X.remove ("string2")
  print (X)

  OUTPUT - ["string1," "string3," "string4"]

- To delete a specific item from the List, the "pop ()" method
  can be used with the position of the value. If no index has
  been indicated, the last item of the index will be removed.
  X = ["string1," "string2," "string3," "string4"]
  X.pop ()
  print (X)

OUTPUT - ["string1," "string2," "string3"]

- To delete a specific index from the List, the "del ()" method can be used followed by the index within square brackets.
  X = ["string1," "string2," "string3," "string4"]
  del X [2]
  print (X)

  OUTPUT - ["string1," "string2," "string4"]

- To delete the entire List variable, the "del ()" method can be used as shown below.
  X = ["string1," "string2," "string3," "string4"]
  del X

  OUTPUT - .....

- To delete all the string values from the List without deleting the variable itself, the "clear ()" method can be used as shown below.
  X = ["string1," "string2," "string3," "string4"]
  X.clear()
  print (X)

  OUTPUT – [ ]

Python Tuples

In Python, Tuples are collections of data types that cannot be changed but can be arranged in specific order. Tuples allow for duplicate items and are written within round brackets, as shown in the syntax below.

Tuple = ("string1," "string2," "string3")
print (Tuple)

Similar to the Python List, you can selectively display desired string from a Tuple by referencing the position of that string inside square bracket in the print command as shown below.

Tuple = ("string1," "string2," "string3")
print (Tuple [1])

OUTPUT – ("string2")

The concept of **negative indexing** can also be applied to Python Tuple, as shown in the example below:
Tuple = ("string1," "string2," "string3," "string4," "string5")
print (Tuple [-2])

OUTPUT – ("string4")

You will also be able to specify a **range of indexes** by indicating the start and end of a range. The result in values of such command on a Python Tuple would be a new Tuple containing only the indicated items, as shown in the example below:

Tuple = ("string1," "string2," "string3," "string4," "string5," "string6")
print (Tuple [1:5])

OUTPUT – *("string2," "string3," "string4," "string5")*

* Remember the first item is at position 0 and the final position of the range, which is the fifth position in this example is not included.

You can also specify a **range of negative indexes** to Python Tuples, as shown in the example below:

Tuple = ("string1," "string2," "string3," "string4," "string5," "string6")
print (Tuple [-4: -2])

OUTPUT – *("string4," "string5")*

* Remember the last item is at position -1 and the final position of this range, which is the negative fourth position in this example is not included in the Output.

Unlike Python Lists, you cannot directly **change the data value of Python Tuples** after they have been created. However, conversion of a Tuple into a List and then modifying the data value of that List will allow you to subsequently create a Tuple from that updated List. Let us look at the example below:

Tuple1 = ("string1," "string2," "string3," "string4," "string5," "string6")
List1 = list (Tuple1)
List1 [2] = "update this list to create new tuple"
Tuple1 = tuple (List1)

print (Tuple1)

OUTPUT – ("string1," "string2," "update this list to create new tuple," "string4," "string5," "string6")

You can also determine the **length** of a Python Tuple using the "len()" function, as shown in the example below:

Tuple = ("string1," "string2," "string3," "string4," "string5," "string6") print (len (Tuple))

OUTPUT – 6

You cannot selectively delete items from a Tuple, but you can use the "del" keyword to **delete the Tuple** in its entirety, as shown in the example below:

Tuple = ("string1," "string2," "string3," "string4")
del Tuple

print (Tuple)

OUTPUT – name 'Tuple' is not defined

You can **join multiple Tuples** with the use of the "+" logical operator.

Tuple1 = ("string1," "string2," "string3," "string4")
Tuple2 = (101, 202, 303)

Tuple3 = Tuple1 + Tuple2
print (Tuple3)

OUTPUT – ("string1," "string2," "string3," "string4," 101, 202, 303)

You can also use the "tuple ( )" constructor to create a Tuple, as shown in the example below:

Tuple1 = tuple (("string1," "string2," "string3," "string4"))
print (Tuple1)

Python Sets

In Python, Sets are collections of data types that cannot be organized and indexed. Sets do not allow for duplicate items and must be written within curly brackets, as shown in the syntax below.

set = {"string1," "string2," "string3"}
print (set)

Unlike the Python List and Tuple, you cannot selectively display desired items from a Set by referencing the position of that item because the Python Set are not arranged in any order, therefore, items do not have any indexing. However, the "for" loop can be used on Sets (more on this topic later in this chapter).

Unlike Python Lists, you cannot directly **change the data values of Python Sets** after they have been created. However, you can use the "add ()" method to add a single item to Set and use the "update ( )" method to one or more items to an already existing Set. Let us look at the example below:

set = {"string1," "string2," "string3"}
set. add ("newstring")
print (set)

OUTPUT – {"string1," "string2," "string3," "newstring"}

set = {"string1," "string2," "string3"}
set. update (["newstring1," "newstring2," "newstring3,")
print (set)

OUTPUT – {"string1," "string2," "string3," "newstring1," "newstring2," "newstring3"}

You can also determine the **length** of a Python Set using the "len()" function, as shown in the example below:

set = {"string1," "string2," "string3," "string4," "string5," "string6," "string7"}
print (len(set))

OUTPUT – 7

To selectively **delete a specific item from a Set**, the "remove ()" method can be used as shown in the code below:

set = {"string1," "string2," "string3," "string4," "string5"}
set. remove ("string4")
print (set)

OUTPUT – {"string1," "string2," "string3," "string5"}

You can also use the "discard ( )" method to delete specific items from a Set, as shown in the example below:

set = {"string1," "string2," "string3," "string4," "string5"}
set. discard ("string3")
print (set)

OUTPUT – {"string1," "string2," "string4," "string5"}
The "pop ( )" method can be used to selectively delete only the last item of a Set. It must be noted here that since the Python Sets are unordered, any item that the system deems as the last item will be removed. As a result, the output of this method will be the item that has been removed.

set = {"string1," "string2," "string3," "string4," "string5"}
A = set.pop ( )
print (A)
print (set)

OUTPUT –
String2
{"string1," "string3," "string4," "string5"}

To delete the entire Set, the "del" keyword can be used as shown below.

set = {"string1," "string2," "string3," "string4," "string5"}

delete set

print (set)

OUTPUT – name 'set' is not defined

To delete all the items from the Set without deleting the variable itself, the "clear ()" method can be used as shown below.

set = {"string1," "string2," "string3," "string4," "string5"}

set.clear ( )

print (set)

OUTPUT – set ( )

You can **join multiple Sets** with the use of the "union ( )" method. The output of this method will be a new Set that contains all items from both the sets. You can also use the "update ( )" method to insert all the items from one set into another without creating a new Set.

Set1 = {"string1," "string2," "string3," "string4," "string5"}

Set2 = {155, 255, 355, 455, 55}

Set3 = Set1.union (Set2)

print (Set3)

OUTPUT – {"string1," 155, "string2," 255, "string3," 355, "string4," 455, "string5," 55}

Set1 = {"string1," "string2," "string3," "string4," "string5"}
Set2 = {155, 255, 355, 455, 55}
Set1.update (Set2)
print (Set1)

OUTPUT – *{255, "string1," 155, "string4,"55, "string2," 355, "string3," 455, "string5"}*

You can also use the "set ( )" constructor to create a Set, as shown in the example below:

Set1 = set (("string1," "string2," "string3," "string4," "string5"))
print (Set1)

OUTPUT – {"string3," "string5," "string2," "string4," "string1"}

Python Dictionary

In Python, Dictionaries are collections of data types that can be changed and indexed but are not arranged in any order. Each item in a Python Dictionary will comprise of a key and its value. Dictionaries do not allow for duplicate items and must be written within curly brackets, as shown in the syntax below.

dict = {
"key01": "value01,"
"key02": "value02,"
"key03": "value03,"
}
print (dict)

You can selectively display desired item value from a Dictionary by referencing to its key inside square brackets in the print command as shown below.

dict = {
"key01": "value01,"
"key02": "value02,"
"key03": "value03,"
}

X = dict ["key02"]

print (X)

OUTPUT – value02

You can also use the "get ( )" method to view the value of a key, as shown in the example below:

dict = {
"key01": "value01,"
"key02": "value02,"
"key03": "value03,"
}

X = dict.get ("key01")
print (X)

OUTPUT – value01

There might be instances when you need to **change the value** of a key in a Python Dictionary. This can be accomplished by referring to the key of that item and declaring the new value. Let us look at the example below:

dict = {
"key01": "value01,"
"key02": "value02,"

"key03": "value03,"
}

dict ["key03"] = "NEWvalue"
print (dict)

OUTPUT – {"key01": "value01," "key02": "value02," "key03": "NEWvalue"}

You can also determine the **length** of a Python Dictionary using the "len()" function, as shown in the example below:

dict = {
"key01": "value01,"
"key02": "value02,"
"key03": "value03,"
"key4": "value4,"
"key5": "value5"
}

print (len (dict))

OUTPUT – 5

Python Dictionary can also be changed by **adding** new index key and assigning a new value to that key, as shown in the example below:

dict = {
"key01": "value01,"
"key02": "value02,"
"key03": "value03,"
}

dict ["NEWkey"] = "NEWvalue"
print (dict)

OUTPUT – {"key01": "value01," "key02": "value02," "key03": "value03," "NEWkey": "NEWvalue"}

There are multiple built-in methods to **delete items** from a Python Dictionary.

- To selectively delete a specific item value, the "pop ()" method can be used with the indicated key name.

  dict = {
  "key01": "value01,"
  "key02": "value02,"
  "key03": "value03,"

}
dict.pop ("key01")
print (dict)

OUTPUT – { "key02": "value02," "key03": "value03"}

- To selectively delete the item value that was last inserted, the "popitem ()" method can be used with the indicated key name.

dict = {
"key01": "value01,"
"key02": "value02,"
"key03": "value03,"
}
dict.popitem ( )
print (dict)

OUTPUT – { "key01": "value01," "key02": "value02"}

- To selectively delete a specific item value, the "del" keyword can also be used with the indicated key name.

dict = {
"key01": "value01,"
"key02": "value02,"

"key03": "value03,"
}
del dict ("key03")
print (dict)

OUTPUT – { "key01": "value01," "key02": "value02"}

- To delete a Python Dictionary in its entirety, the "del" keyword can also be used as shown in the example below:

dict = {
"key01": "value01,"
"key02": "value02,"
"key03": "value03,"
}
del dict
print (dict)

OUTPUT – name 'dict' is not defined

- To delete all the items from the Dictionary without deleting the Dictionary itself, the "clear ()" method can be used as shown below.

dict = {
"key01": "value01,"

"key02": "value02,"

"key03": "value03,"

}

dict.clear ( )

print (dict)

OUTPUT – { }

There might be instances when you need to **copy** an existing Python Dictionary. This can be accomplished by using the built-in "copy ( )" method or the "dict ( )" method, as shown in the examples below:

dict = {

"key01": "value01,"

"key02": "value02,"

"key03": "value03,"

}

newdict = dict.copy ( )

print (newdict)

OUTPUT – {"key01": "value01," "key02": "value02," "key03": "value03"}

Olddict = {

"key01": "value01,"

"key02": "value02,"
"key03": "value03,"
}
newdict = dict (Olddict)
print (newdict)

OUTPUT – {"key01": "value01," "key02": "value02," "key03": "value03"}

There is a unique feature that supports multiple Python Dictionaries to be **nested** within another Python Dictionary. You can either create a Dictionary containing child Dictionaries, as shown in the example below:

```
McManiaFamilyDict = {
       "burger1" : {
               "name" : "VegWrap,"
               "price" : 3.99
       },
       "burger2" : {
               "name" : "Burger,"
               "price" : 6
       },
       "burger3" : {
               "name" : "CheeseBurger,"
               "price" : 2.99
```

```
        }
}
print (McManiaFamilyDict)
```

OUTPUT - {"burger1" : { "name" : "VegWrap," "price" : 3.99}, "burger2" : {"name" : "Burger," "price" : 6}, "burger3" : {"name" : "CheeseBurger," "price" : 2.99}}

Alternatively, you can create a brand new Dictionary that contain other Dictionaries already existing on the system, your code will look like the one below:

```
burgerDict1 : {
        "name" : "VegWrap,"
        "price" : 3.99
}

burgerDict2 : {
        "name" : "Burger,"
        "price" : 6
}

burgerDict3 : {
        "name" : "CheeseBurger,"
        "price" : 2.99
}
```

```
McManiaFamilyDict = {
        "burgerDict1" : burgerDict1,
        "burgerDict2" : burgerDict2
        "burgerDict3" : burgerDict3
}
print (McManiaFamilyDict)
```

OUTPUT - {"burger1" : { "name" : "VegWrap," "price" : 3.99}, "burger2" : {"name" : "Burger," "price" : 6}, "burger3" : {"name" : "CheeseBurger," "price" : 2.99}}

Lastly, you can use the "dict ( )" function to create a new Python Dictionary. The key differences when you create items for the Dictionary using this function are: 1. Round brackets are used instead of the curly brackets. 2. Equal to sign is used instead of the semi-colon. Let us look at the example below:

DictwithFunction = dict (key1 = "value1," key2 = "value2," key3 = "value3")
print (DictwithFunction)

OUTPUT – {"key1": "value1," "key2": "value2," "key3": "value3"}

Chapter 4: Neural Network and Predictive Analysis

Neural Network

The programming of computers needs a human programmer. Humans to instruct a computer to provide solutions to our problems use many lines of code. However, the computer can attempt to fix the issue itself through machine learning and neural networks. A neural network is "a function that learns the expected output for a given input from training datasets." For instance, you can train the neural network with many sample pictures to construct a neural network that recognizes pictures of a bear. The resulting network operates as a functionality to generate the "bear" label as output for the bear picture input. Another more convenient example would be training the neural network using multiple user activity logs from gaming servers and generate an output stating which users are very likely to convert to paying customer.

The "Neural Network" features only a single neuron, also called "perceptron." It is a straightforward and fundamental mechanism, which can be implemented with basic math. The primary distinction between traditional programming and a neural network is that computers running on neural network learn from the provided training data set to determine the parameters (weights and prejudice) on their own, without needing any human assistance. Algorithms like "back propagation" and "gradient descent" may be used to train the parameters. It can be stated that the computer tries to increase or decrease every parameter a bit, in the hope that the optimal combination of Parameters can be found, to minimize the error compared with training data set.

Fundamentals of Neural Network

- Neural networks need clear and informative big data to be trained. You can think of Neural networks as a toddler. They start by observing how their parents are walking. Then they attempt to walk on their own, and the kid learns how to accomplish future tasks with every step. Similarly, the Neural network may fail a few times, but it learns how to generate desired predictions after a few failing attempts.

- For complicated issues such as image processing, it is advisable to use Neural Networks. Neural networks belong to a group of algorithms called "representation learning algorithms." These algorithms are capable of simplifying complicated issues by generating simple (or "representative") form, which tends to be more difficult for conventional (non-representation) algorithms.

- To determine what type of neural network model is suitable for solving the issue at hand, let the data dictate how you fix the issue. For instance, "recurring neural networks" are more appropriate if the issue pertains to sequence generation. While it might be better for you to use "convolutional neural networks" to solve an image-related issue.

- In order to run a deep neural network model, hardware specifications are vital. Neural networks have been around for a long time now, but they are recently experiencing an upsurge primarily credited to the fact that computer resources today are better and more effective. If you want to address a real-life problem using neural network, it is wise to purchase high-end hardware.

TensorFlow

TensorFlow can be defined as a Machine Learning platform providing end-to-end service with a variety of free and open-sources. It has a system of multilayered nodes that allow for quick building, training and deployment of artificial neural networks with large data sets. It is touted as a "simple and flexible architecture to take new ideas from concept to code to state-of-the-art models and to publication at a rapid pace." For example, Google uses TensorFlow libraries in their image recognition and speech recognition tools and technologies.

Higher-level APIs such as "tf.estimator" can be used for specifying predefined architectures, such as "linear regressors" or "neural networks." The picture below shows existing hierarchy of the TensorFlow tool kit:

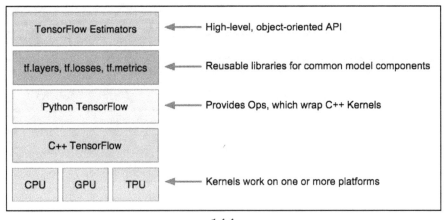

The picture shown below provides the purposes of the different layers:

Toolkit(s)	Description
Estimator (tf.estimator)	High-level, OOP API.
tf.layers/tf.losses/tf.metrics	Libraries for common model components.
TensorFlow	Lower-level APIs

The two fundamental components of TensorFlow are:
1. A "graph protocol buffer"
2. A "runtime" that can execute the graph

The two components mentioned above are similar to "Python" code and the "Python interpreter." Just as "Python interpreter" can run Python code on several hardware systems, TensorFlow can be operated on various hardware systems, like CPU, GPU, and TPU.

To make a decision regarding which API(s) should be used, you must consider the API offering the highest abstraction level to solve the target problem. Easier to use, but (by design) less flexible, are the greater abstract levels. It is recommended to first begin with the highest-level API and make everything work. If for certain unique modelling issues, you need extra flexibility, move

145

one level down. Notice that each level is constructed on the lower level APIs. It should thus be quite simple to decrease the hierarchy.

For the development of majority of Machine Learning models, we will use "tf.estimator" API, which significantly lowers the number of code lines needed for development. In addition, "tf.estimator" is compatible with Scikit-Learn API.

Training a Neural Network using TensorFlow

In this exercise, we will develop a model of neural networks for classifying clothing images such as sneakers and shirts, using TensorFlow library.

I – Import the dataset

For this example, we will be using "Fashion MNIST" data set with 60,000 pictures representing 10 different categories. The low-resolution pictures (28 to 28 pixels) indicate individual clothing items. For the classic MNIST dataset, "Fashion MNIST" is intended as a drop-in replacement. The "MNIST" data set includes pictures of handwritten numbers (0, 1, and so on.) in the same format as the clothing items used in this example. To train the network, we will use 60,000 pictures and 10,000 pictures will be used to assess the accuracy with which the network has learned how to classify pictures.

The "Fashion MNIST" data set is accessible directly from TensorFlow, using the import command as below:
"fashion_mnist = keras.datasets.fashion_mnist (train_images, train_labels), (test_images, test_labels) = fashion_mnist.load_data()"

After the dataset has been loaded, system will return 4 different "NumPy arrays" including:
- The *"train_images"* and *"train_labels"* arrays, which serve as the "training dataset" for the model.
- The *"test_images"* and *"test_labels"* arrays, which serve as the "testing dataset" that the model can be tested against.'

Now we need to create labels for an array of integers (0 to 9), corresponding to each category/class of the clothing picture in the data set, using command below, which will look like the table, represented in the picture below. This will be useful in generating predictions using our model.

"class_names = ['T-shirt/top,' 'Trouser,' 'Pullover,' 'Dress,' 'Coat,' 'Sandal,' 'Shirt,' 'Sneaker,' 'Bag,' 'Ankle boot']"

Label	Class
0	T-shirt/top
1	Trouser
2	Pullover
3	Dress
4	Coat
5	Sandal
6	Shirt
7	Sneaker
8	Bag
9	Ankle boot

II – Data Exploration

To get some sense of the data set, it can be explored using commands listed below:

To view the total number of images in the "training data set" and the size of each image – "*train_images.shape*," which will produce the output displayed as "(60000, 28, 28)" stating we have 60,000 pictures of 28 to 28 pixel size.

To view the total number of labels in the "training dataset" – "*len(train_labels)*," which will produce the output displayed as "60000" stating we have 60,000 labels in the training data set.

To view the data type of each label used in the "training dataset"– "*train_labels*," which will produce the output displayed as "*array([9, 0, 0, ..., 3, 0, 5], dtype=uint8)*" stating each label is an integer between 0 and 9.

To view the total number of images in the "testing dataset" and the size of each image – "*test_images.shape*," which will produce the output displayed as "(10000, 28, 28)" stating we have 10,000 pictures of 28 to 28 pixel size in the testing data set.

To view the total number of labels in the "testing dataset" – "*len(test_labels)*," which will produce the output displayed as "10000" stating we have 10,000 labels in the testing data set.

III – Data Pre-processing

To make the data suitable for training the model, it needs to be pre-processed. It is essential to pre-process the data sets to be used for training and testing in the same manner.

For instance, you notice the first picture in the training data set has the pixel values between 0 and 255, using the commands below:

"*plt.figure()*"
"*plt.imshow(train_images[0])*"
"*plt.colorbar()*"
"*plt.grid(False)*"
"*plt.show()*"

These pixel values need to be scaled to fall between 0 to 1, prior to being used as input for the Neural Network model. Therefore, the values need to be divided by 255, for both the data subsets, using commands below:

"train_images   =   train_images   /   255.0"
"test_images = test_images / 255.0"

The final pre-processing step here would be to make sure that the data is desired format prior to building the Neural Network by viewing the first 20 pictures from the training dataset and displaying the "class name" under each picture, using commands below:

"plt.figure(figsize=(10,10))"
"for   i   in   range(20):
                                        plt.subplot(5,5,i+1)
                                        plt.xticks([])
                                        plt.yticks([])
                                        plt.grid(False)
            plt.imshow(train_images[i],   cmap=plt.cm.binary)
                    plt.xlabel(class_names[train_labels[i]])"
"plt.show()"

IV – Building the Neural Network Model

To build up the "Neural Network," the constituting layers of the model first need to be configured and only then, the model can be compiled.

Configuring the Layers

The "layers" are the fundamental construction block of a neural network. These "layers" take out information from the data entered generating representations that tend to be extremely valuable addressing the problem.

Majority of "deep learning" involves stacking and linking fundamental layers together. The parameters that are learned during practice are available in most of the layers, like "tf.keras.layers.Dense." To configure the required layers, use command below:

"model   =   keras.Sequential([
keras.layers.Flatten(input_shape=(28,   28)),
keras.layers.Dense(128,   activation=tf.nn.relu),
keras.layers.Dense(10,   activation=tf.nn.softmax)
])"

The *"tf.keras.layers.Flatten"* is the first layer in this network, which turns the picture format from a 2-dimesnional array of 28x28 size to a 1-dimension array with "28x28 = 784" pixels. Consider this layer as unchained rows of pixels in the picture that arranged these pictures but without any learning parameters and capable of only altering the data.

The network comprises of couple of *"tf.keras.layers.Dense"* layers after pixels are flattened. These neural layers are fully or densely connected. There are 128 nodes or neurons in the first Dense layer. The succeeding and final layer is a 10-node layer of "*Softmax,*" which generated an array of ten different probability scores amounting to "1." Every single node includes a probability score indicating that one of the ten classes is likely to contain the existing picture.

Compiling the Model

Before being able to train the model, some final tweaks are needed to be made in the model compilation step, such as:

Loss function— This provides a measure of the model's accuracy during training. This feature should be minimized, so that the model is "directed" in the correct direction.

Optimizer —These are the updates made to the model based on the data it can view as well as its "loss function."

Metrics — Used for monitoring the training and testing procedures. For example, the code below utilizes accuracy, measured by computing the fraction of the pictures that were classified accurately.

"model.compile(optimizer='adam,'

loss='sparse_categorical_crossentropy,'

metrics=['accuracy'])"

V – Training the Model

The steps listed below are used to train the "Neural Network Model":

- Feed the training data to the model, using *"train_images"* and *"train_labels"* arrays.

- Allow the network to learn association of pictures and corresponding labels.

- Generate predictions using the model for a predefined test date set, for example, the *"test_images"* array. Then the predictions must be verified by matching the labels from the *"test_labels"* array.

You can begin to train the network, by utilizing the *"model.fit"* method. To verify the system is a "fit" for the training data, use command *"model.fit(train_images, train_labels, epochs=5)."*

The epochs are displayed as below, suggesting that the model has reached accuracy of around 0.89 or 89% of the training data:

"Epoch 1/5

60000/60000 [==============================] - 4s 75us/sample - loss: 0.5018 - acc: 0.8241

Epoch 2/5

*60000/60000 [==============================] - 4s
71us/sample - loss: 0.3763 - acc: 0.8643*

Epoch 3/5

*60000/60000 [==============================] - 4s
71us/sample - loss: 0.3382 - acc: 0.8777*

Epoch 4/5

*60000/60000 [==============================] - 4s
72us/sample - loss: 0.3138 - acc: 0.8846*

Epoch 5/5

*60000/60000 [==============================] - 4s
72us/sample - loss: 0.2967 - acc: 0.8897*

*<tensorflow.python.keras.callbacks.History   at
0x7f65fb64b5c0>"*

VI – Measuring the accuracy of the Neural Network Model

To test the accuracy of the network, it must be verified against the testing data set using commands below:

"test_loss, test_acc = model.evaluate(test_images, test_labels)"

"print('Test accuracy:,' test_acc)"

The output can be obtained as shown below, which suggests that the accuracy of the test result is around 0.86 or 86%, which is slightly less that the accuracy of the training data set. This is a classic example of "overfitting," when the performance or accuracy of the model is lower on new input or testing data than the training data.

"10000/10000 [==============================] - 1s 51us/sample - loss: 0.3653 - acc: 0.8671

Test accuracy: 0.8671"

VII – Generate predictions using the Neural Network Model

Now that our model has been trained sufficiently, we are ready to generate predictions from the model, using command *"predictions = model.predict(test_images)."*

In the code below, the network has generated a prediction for labels of each picture in the testing data set. The prediction is generated as an array of ten integers with the "confidence" index for each of the ten categories (refer the import data stage) corresponding to the test picture.

"predictions[0]"

"array([6.58371528e-06,   1.36480646e-10,   4.17183337e-08, 1.15178166e-10,

8.30939484e-07,   1.49914682e-01,   3.11488043e-06, 4.63472381e-02,

6.10820061e-05, 8.03666413e-01], dtype=float32)"

To view the label with the highest "confidence" index, using command *"np.argmax (predictions[0])."*

A result "9," will suggest that the model has maximum confidence on the test image belonging to *"class_names[9]"* or according to our labels table, ankle boot. To verify this prediction, use command *"test_labels[0],"* which should generate output as "9."

To view the whole set of predictions for the ten classes, use command below:

"def plot_image(i, predictions_array, true_label, img):
 predictions_array, true_label, img = predictions_array[i], true_label[i],   img[i]
plt.grid(False)
plt.xticks([])
plt.yticks([])

plt.imshow(img,   cmap=plt.cm.binary)

```python
  predicted_label = np.argmax(predictions_array)
  if predicted_label == true_label:
    color = 'blue'
  else:
    color = 'red'

  plt.xlabel('{} {:2.0f}% ({}).'format(class_names[predicted_label],
                                100*np.max(predictions_array),
                                class_names[true_label]),
                                color=color)

def plot_value_array(i, predictions_array, true_label):
  predictions_array, true_label = predictions_array[i], true_label[i]
  plt.grid(False)
  plt.xticks([])
  plt.yticks([])
  thisplot = plt.bar(range(10), predictions_array, color='#777777')
  plt.ylim([0, 1])
  predicted_label = np.argmax(predictions_array)

  thisplot[predicted_label].set_color('red')
  thisplot[true_label].set_color('blue')"
```

Now, for example, you may want to generate a prediction for a specific picture in the testing data set. You can do this using the command below:

"Grab an image from the test dataset
img = test_images[0]
print(img.shape)"

"(28, 28)"

To use the "tf.keras" models to generate this prediction, the picture must be added to a list, since these models have been optimized to generate predictions on a "collection of dataset" at a time. Use command below to accomplish this:

"# Add the image to a batch where it's the only member.
img = (np.expand_dims(img,0))

print(img.shape)"

"(1, 28, 28)"

Now, to generate the prediction for the picture using "tf.keras" use the command below:

"predictions_single = model.predict(img)
print(predictions_single)"

The predictions generated will resemble the code below:

"[[6.5837266e-06 1.3648087e-10 4.1718483e-08 1.1517859e-10 8.3093937e-07

1.4991476e-01 3.1148918e-06 4.6347316e-02 6.1082108e-05 8.0366623e-01]]"

To generate a graph or plot for the prediction (as shown in the picture below), use command below:

"plot_value_array(0, predictions_single, test_labels) plt.xticks(range(10), class_names, rotation=45) plt.show()"

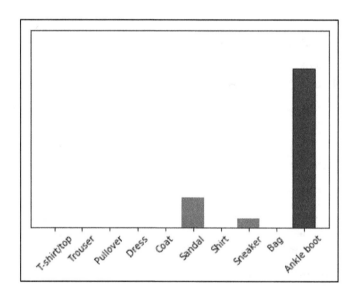

The *"model.predict"* generated the output as a "list of lists," for every single picture in the testing data set. To generate predictions specifically for the specific image we used earlier, use command below:

"prediction_result = np.argmax(predictions_single[0]) print(prediction_result)"

The output or prediction generated should be "9" as we obtained earlier.

Applications of the Machine Learning Technology

Virtual Personal Assistants

The most popular examples of virtual personal assistance are Siri and Alexa. These systems are capable of providing relevant information using simple voice commands. Machine learning is at the heart of these devices and systems, as they collect and define the information generated with every user interaction and use this information as training data to learn user preferences and provide enhanced experience.

Predictions While Driving

Most of the vehicles today are utilizing GPS navigation services, which collects information such as our current location, and driving speed on a centralized server that can be used to generate a map of current traffic. This helps in managing traffic and reducing congestion. With the use of machine learning, system can estimate the regions where and the time of the day when traffic jams occur frequently. Machine learning algorithms allow ride sharing services such as Lyft and Uber, to minimize detours on their routes and provides users an upfront estimate of how much the ride will cost.

Video Surveillance

Machines have taken over the monotonous job of monitoring multiple video cameras to ensure security of premises. Machines can track unusual behavior like standing motionless for extended period, sleeping on benches and stumbling. It can then send an alert to the security personnel who can make the final decision to act on the tip and avoid mishaps. With every iteration of reporting, the surveillance services are improved as the machine learning algorithms learn and improve upon itself.

Social Media

Social media platforms such as "Facebook," "Twitter" and "Instagram" are using machine learning algorithms to train the system from user activity and behavior to be able to provide engaging and enhanced user experience. Some of the examples of the functionalities that are being driven by machine learning algorithms are "People you may know" feature on Facebook (that collects and learns from user activities such as the profiles they visit often, they're own profile and their friends to suggest other Facebook users that they can become friends with) and "Similar Pins" feature on Pinterest (that is driven by computer vision Technology working in tandem with machine learning to identify objects in the images of user's saved "pins" and recommend similar "pins" accordingly).

Email Spam and Malware Filtering

All email clients such as Gmail, Yahoo Mail and Hotmail use machine learning algorithms to ascertain that the spam filter functionality is continuously updated and cannot be penetrated by spammers and malware. Some of the spam filtering techniques that are powered by machine learning are Multi Layered Perceptron and C 4.5 decision tree induction.

Online Customer Service

Nowadays most of the e-commerce sites provide users with an option to chat with at customer service representative, which are usually supported by a Chatbot instead of a live executive. These bots use machine learning technology to understand user inquiries and extract information from the website in order to be able to resolve customer issues. With every interaction, Chatbots become smarter and more humanlike.

Refinement of Search Engine Results

Search engines such as "Google," "Yahoo" and "Bing" use machine learning algorithms to provide improved search results pertinent with the user provided keywords. For every search result, the algorithm observes and learns from user activity such as opening suggested links and the order in which the opened link was displayed as well as time spent on the opened link. This helps the search engine to understand which search results more optimal and any modifications needed to further improve the search results.

Product Recommendations

The product recommendation feature has now become the heart and soul of online shopping experience. Machine learning algorithms in combination with artificial intelligence fuel the product recommendation functionality. The system observes and learns from consumer activity and behavior such as past purchases, wish list, recently viewed items and liked or added to cart items.

Online Fraud Detection

The financial institutions are relying heavily on machine learning algorithms and artificial intelligence to make cyber space secure by tracking potentially fraudulent monetary transactions online. For example, PayPal is using Machine learning algorithms to prevent money laundering through its platform. They are using a set of artificial intelligence tools in combination with Machine learning algorithms to analyze millions of transactions and distinguish between legitimate and illegitimate transactions between the buyer and the seller. With every transaction, the system learns which transactions are legitimate and which transactions could be potentially fraudulent.

Predictive Analytics

According to SAS, predictive analytics is *"use of data, statistical algorithms and machine learning techniques to identify the likelihood of future outcomes based on historical data. The goal is to go beyond knowing what has happened to provide a best assessment of what will happen in the future."* Today companies are digging through their past with an eye on the future and this is where artificial intelligence for marketing comes into play, with the application of predictive analytics technology. The success of the predictive analytics is directly proportional to the quality of big data collected by the company.

Here are some of the widely used predictive analytics applications for marketing:

Predictive Analysis for Customer Behavior

For the industrial giants like "Amazon," "Apple" and "Netflix" analyzing customer activities and behavior is fundamental to their day-to-day operations. Smaller businesses are increasingly assuming their role to implement predictive analysis in their business model. Development of customized suite of predictive models for a company is not only capital-intensive but also requires extensive manpower and time. Marketing companies like "AgilOne" offer relatively simple predictive model types with wide applicability across industrial domains. They have identified three main types of predictive models to analyze customer behavior, which are:

"Propensity models" – These models are used to generate "true or accurate" predictions for customer behavior. Some of the most common propensity models include: "predictive lifetime value," "propensity to buy," "propensity to turn," "propensity to convert," "likelihood of engagement" and "propensity to unsubscribe."

"Cluster models" – These models are used to separate, and group customers based on shared attributes such as gender, age, purchase history and demographics. Some of the most common cluster models include "product based or category base clustering," "behavioral customs clustering" and "brand based clustering."

"Collaborative filtering" – These models are used to generate product and services and recommendations as well as to recommended advertisements based on prior customer activities and behaviors. Some of the most common collaborative filtering models include "up sell," "cross sell" and "next sell" recommendations.

The most significant tool used by companies to execute predictive analytics on customer behavior is "regression analysis," which allows the company to establish correlations between sale of a particular product and the specific attributes displayed by the purchasing customer. This is achieved by employing "regression coefficients," which are numeric values depicting the degree to which the customer behavior is affected by different variables and developing a "likelihood score" for future sale of the product.

Qualification and Prioritization of Leads

There are three primary categories employed in business-to-business or B2B predictive analytics marketing to qualify and prioritize prospective customers or "leads."

These categories are:

- **"Predictive scoring"** which is used to prioritize prospective customers on the basis of their likelihood to make an actual purchase

- **"Identification models"** which are used to identify and acquire new prospective customers based on attributes that are shared with the existing customers of the company.

- **"Automated segmentation"** which is used to separate and classify prospective customers based on shared attributes to be targeted with same personalized marketing strategies and campaigns.

The predictive analytics technology needs large volume of sales data that serves as a building block and training material to increase in the accuracy and efficiency of the predictive models. Small brick-and-mortar companies cannot afford to expand their computing resources, therefore, are unable to efficiently collect customer behavioral data from their in-store sales. This translates into a competitive edge for the larger companies with more advanced computing system, which exacerbates the superfluous growth of larger companies in comparison to small businesses.

Identification of Current Market Trends

Companies can employ "data visualization" tools that allow business executives and managers to gather insights on the current state of the company, simply by visualizing their existing customer behavioral data on a "report or dashboard." These dashboard reports tend to inspire and generate customer behavior driven actions. For example, with the use of data visualization tools a company can identify the underlying trend of customer demands in specific neighborhoods and accordingly plan to stock their inventory for individual stores. The same information can bring to light the best products and services for the company to be launched based on the current market trends that can suffice the customer demands. The market trend insights can also be applied to increase the efficiency of company's supply chain management model.

Customer Segmentation and Targeting

One of the simplest and highly effective way of optimizing a product offer to achieve a rapid turnaround on company's return on investment is the ability to target "right customers" with appropriate product offers at the "right time." This also happens to be the most common and widely used application of predictive analytics in the world of marketing. According to a research study conducted by the "Aberdeen Group," companies using predictive analytics in their marketing strategies are two times more likely to successfully identify "high value customers." This is where the quality of company's existing data set takes precedence. The highly recommended practice is to use historical consumer behavioral data of all existing customers, analyze it to segment, and target customers with similar purchasing attributes with a personalized recommendations and marketing campaigns.

Some of the most common predictive analytics models used and this application are "affinity analysis," "churn analysis" and "response modeling." Using these applications, companies can gather insight such as "if combining digital and print subscriptions of their product offerings or catalog is a good idea" or "whether their product or service will be more successful if offered as a monthly subscription model or one-time purchase fee." One of the leading sales and marketing platform companies is "Salesforce," which offers a cloud-based platform that can be used by businesses to generate customer profiles as a product of the data collected from independent sources, including customer relationship management (CRM) applications and other company applications. By selectively and mindfully adding inputted data to this platform, companies can seamlessly track their customer behavior to develop a customer behavioral model overtime that can feed into company's decision-making process in real time and over long term.

Development of Marketing Strategies

Another application of predictive analytics and marketing is providing access to a variety of customer-related data such as data collected from social media platforms and companies own internal structured data. The customer behavioral model can then be generated by collating all available data and applying "behavioral scoring" on it. All the companies across different industrial sectors are required to adapt to changing or evolving customer behavior through proliferating marketing mediums or channels. For example, companies can use any of the predictive analytics model described above, to precisely predict if their planned marketing campaign would have more success on the social media platforms or on their mobile applications.

Companies are able to employ predictive analytics model to gain an understanding of how their customers are interacting with their products or services, based on their feelings or emotions shared on the social media platforms concerning a particular topic. This process is referred to as "sentiment analysis" or "text analysis."

Exploratory Analysis of Customer Data

"Exploratory Data Analysis" or EDA provides a comprehensive view of existing customer data generated pertinent customer data sources such as product prices, current and historical customer surveys, product usage, purchase history and demographics. It is considered as an approach to look at the data without the use of any statistical model and the data inferences. John Tukey coined the term "Exploratory Data Analysis", in his book released in 1977. Some of the main reasons to use exploratory data analysis are:

- Preliminary selection of the applicable "predictive models."
- Verification of underlying assumptions.
- Make sure company is asking the right questions to expand their customer base.
- Detect potential data anomalies, redundancies and errors.
- Determination of relationship between the "explanatory variables."
- Assessment of the direction and size of relationship between "explanatory variables" and "outcome variables."

The customer data collected in the database form of a rectangular array with individual columns for "subject identifier," "outcome variable" and "explanatory variable." It is rather challenging to look at a spreadsheet filled with numerical values and determine important information from the data and this is where exploratory data analysis techniques are used to selectively display important character is to of the data. There are four types of exploratory data analysis techniques:

1. **"Univariate non-graphical"** - This technique looks at a single variable or data column at a time and displays the results as a statistical summary.

2. **"Multivariate non- graphical"** - This technique looks at two or more variables or data columns at a time and displays the results as a statistical summary.

3. **"Univariate graphical"** - This technique looks at a single variable or data column at a time and displays the results diagrammatically or using pictorial graphs.

4. **"Multivariate graphical"** - This technique looks at two or more variables or data columns at a time and displays the results diagrammatically or using pictorial graphs.

EDA helps in determination of the best predictive model to address the business problem by generating a low risk and low-cost comprehensive report of the data findings and solution recommendations for best suited customer data models. The in-depth exploratory analysis of customer behavior provides exposure to hidden data patterns and market trends that would have been easily lost in the mass of information.

Some of the conclusions that can be derived using of EDA on customer behavioral data are:

- Identification of customers with highest number of purchases and maximum amount of money spent.
- Finding the number of orders generated on a daily, weekly and monthly basis.
- Identification of the distribution of the unit price for all company products.
- Identify purchase transaction patterns based on demographics and location of the customers.

Personalized Marketing with Artificial Intelligence

In a research study sponsored by "Researchscape International," about 75% the marketing agencies stated that personalize marketing has immensely held their companies and clients in advancing customer relationships and a whopping 97% stated that they would continue to invest in personalized marketing efforts. This is primarily driven by the fact that companies are able to effectively communicate with their target markets, by gathering valuable insights from customer behavioral data using predictive analytics and machine learning algorithms. Typically, personalization starts from an individual customer but can potentially be applied to a segment of customers with shared attributes and achieve "personalization at scale." Artificial intelligence-based tools and applications can perform image recognition and voice analysis in combination with customer behavior analysis to provide companies a deeper understanding of customer demands and needs that can be met by delivering precise product recommendations.

Here are some industrial applications of personalized marketing:

Ad Targeting

Companies can target advertisements to a specific user or a segment of customers based on their shopping attributes such as recent views of a particular product or category and purchase history. Some of the Ad targeting applications available in the market are:

"ReFUEL4" – The "Ad Analyzer," developed by the marketing company "ReFUEL4," utilizes computer's visual capabilities to predict the performance of advertisement. If the company's existing ad starts declining in performance, the ad analyzer can help the company to develop a new and better ad. The decline in ad performance typically signals audience fatigue, when people stop paying attention to the ad because it has become too familiar and uninteresting.

"Match2one" – This advertising application can be integrated to the company's e-commerce site and used to I have tracked prospective customers and retain existing customers. The "Match2One" application uses machine learning algorithms to target potential customers that have a higher likelihood paying consumers. The company claims that it's "engine is trained to generate leads and find new customers using a combination of site visitor behavior and historical data." By analyzing the website visitor data, the application can show targeted ads to the customers hold displayed interest and in particular product.

Personalized Messaging

The most important aspect of personalized messaging is contextual marketing. To make sure relevant messages are being sent to the target audience, companies gather customer data including their behavior, webpage view history, preferred content, social media posts and demographics among other variables. Some of the personalized messaging application available in the market are:

"Dynamic yield" – The email solution provided by the company uses customer behavioral data such as order history, email clicks, social media activity among other features to generate personalized email content for the individual customers. The email solution supplies dynamic email templates then can be easily customized to reflect relevant messages. This application is used across several industrial domains including travel, E-commerce, gaming industry and social media.

"Yoochoose" – This company offers e-commerce services to online retailers that allows the company to create a "personalized shopping experience" for their consumers, using personalized emails or targeted notifications with newsletters and product recommendations that automatically triggered buy customer behavior. The application is capable of identifying customers who have not made a purchase for some time and trigger a notification to remind them to make a purchase. It can also identify customers who have recently made a purchase and trigger an "after sale thank you" email. The company offers the "target notifications" functionality along with a product recommendation engine and a "personalized search," all of which are packaged into a "personalization suite."

Product Recommendations

The easiest and smartest read for any company to grow their business is to provide accurate product recommendations that are relevant to the needs and demands of the customer. Companies can also reduce the volume and frequency of product returns while increasing their income through new products, repeat purchases and retargeting to entice new potential customers and higher customer loyalty. Some of the product recommendations applications available in the market are:

"Recombee" – This application is based on advance machine learning algorithms that are capable of generating recommendations within "200 millisecond of the customer activity." The company claims that its application can generate over 500 recommendations per second, by employing a combination of "collaborative filtering algorithms" developed for customer behavioral analysis and "content-based algorithms" to analyze product titles and descriptions. With every human interaction the learning algorithms improves upon itself and continues to refine the recommendations with iterative use by the customer. This application is widely used in real estate industry, job boards, classified ad, gaming industry, travel industry and entertainment industry, among others.

"Sentient Aware" – The product recommendation engine offered by "Sentient Aware" analyzes consumer's Visual activity and behavioral interactions to activate the "deep learning algorithms" within the company website. This application utilizes "intent and curation driven algorithms" to identify similar products and the company catalog to generate predictions on customers Preferences and make product recommendations that align with those preferences. The company claims that its application is just as efficient at recommending products for first-time users owing to its capability to generate recommendations without using historical data.

Dynamic Websites

A website that can cater to individual site preferences of every customer on-the-fly, by dynamically changing its content, which is driven by underlying scripts is called a "dynamic website." The repetitive tasks including tagging photos and rendering photos are carried out using artificial intelligence technologies such as "image recognition" and "machine learning." Some of the dynamic website applications available in the market today are:

"Bookmark" – The company "Bookmark" has successfully applied Machine learning technology to web design. The company claims that its "AI Design Assistant" or (AIDA) can custom build company websites pertaining to various website elements, sections and images as well as the overall web design that should feature on the site based on the company's industry specific information. "AIDA" is capable of searching the Internet to gather more information about the client company by running a search on the company name location and type of business. This application collects information on client's customer behavior and activity on social media and analyzes that information to determine the best website elements and design for the company's e-commerce platform.

"LiftIgniter" –The dynamic website recommendation system developed by "LiftIgniter," can be directly integrated with the client's e-commerce platforms online and on mobile applications and is driven by the machine learning algorithm called "true parallel multivariate algorithms infrastructure." This integrated system learns from the customer interactions with the e-commerce platforms and sifts through all of company's online content to display recommended products within 150 milliseconds that the customer might be interested in, based on their real time activity on the platform.

Conclusion

Thank you for making it through to the end of **Machine Learning with Python** - *The Ultimate Guide to Learn Machine Learning Algorithms. Includes a Useful Section about Analysis, Data Mining and Artificial Intelligence in Business Applications*, let's hope it was informative and able to provide you with all of the tools you need to achieve your goals whatever they may be.

The next step is to make the best use of your new-found wisdom of Python programming, data science, data analysis, and machine learning that have resulted in the birth of the powerhouse, which is the "Silicon Valley." Businesses across the industrial spectrum with an eye on the future are gradually turning into big technology companies under the shadow of their intended business model. This has been proven with the rise of the "FinTech" industry attributed to the financial institutions and enterprises across the world. This book is filled with real-life examples to help you understand the practical details of the underlying concepts along with the names and descriptions of multiple tools that you can further explore and selectively implement to make sound choices for development of a desired machine learning model. Now that you have finished reading this book and mastered the use of Python programming, you are all set to start developing your own Python based machine learning model as well as performing big data analysis using all the open-sources readily available and explicitly described in this book. You can position yourself to use your deep knowledge and understanding of all the cutting-edge technologies obtained from this book to contribute to the growth of any company and land yourself a new high paying and rewarding job!

Finally, if you found this book useful in any way, a review on Amazon is always appreciated!

www.ingramcontent.com/pod-product-compliance
Lightning Source LLC
La Vergne TN
LVHW051234050326
832903LV00028B/2400